The Faith Translation
NEW TESTAMENT
FROM GALATIANS TO JUDE

ONE BODY
Braided Together
COMMEMORATIVE EDITION

info@thefaithtranslation.com
thefaithtranslation.com

Scan here to download our mobile app.

The Faith Publishing
967 Prescott Blvd
Deltona, FL 32738

ISBN 978-1-7358215-6-6

This is a commemorative edition of The Faith Translation that was compiled and printed to celebrate our gathering as One body braided together in Christ, the Word of Eternal life, and the hope of the same life and immortality in our flesh, when we shall appear in His life and likeness in the power of the resurrection.

Thank you, Father, for all who speak, all who participate and for all who came to fellowship around Your life. Amen.

TABLE OF CONTENTS

The Faith Translation Mission

The Faith Translation's mission is to translate the scriptures, by expounding upon and emphasizing the faith of Jesus Christ that is contained in all the scripture. And to distribute this translation free to as many in the world as possible.

You may be wondering, why do we need another bible translation?

I have long thought that if Jesus said that there is only one thing needful, and He did. And that One thing was to hear and keep on hearing to the faith of Jesus Christ;

To harken diligently to the faith of Jesus, the faith that was from the beginning and was made immortal flesh in Him in the resurrection from the dead.

Then, I thought if I were to do a bible translation there is only one thing needful to bring out of the scriptures, The Faith that was authored and finished by Jesus Christ. And that is exactly what I felt led to do.

It is from these thoughts that The Faith Translation was born and in late 2020 the first book was completed.

I see so much confusion in the world and even the church today regarding God, but Jesus said He came to reveal the Father's heart for us all.

There are 45,000+ denominations worldwide but the scripture says there is One Faith: The Faith of the Son of God.

The word faith means "be persuaded." And the most vital thing anyone can hear and be persuaded of is the faith of Jesus Christ, the faith of the Son of God. Because this has been God's message to mankind from the beginning and throughout the scriptures, Old and New Testament.

The Apostle Paul asks a very important question to the Galatians. He said, this only would I ask you; did you receive the Spirit by the works of the law or the hearing of faith?

Of course, the answer is that it is only by hearing the faith that one receives the Spirit. The same Spirit that raised Jesus from the dead immortal. The same Spirit that produces the fruit of love, joy, peace, patience, kindness, goodness, faithfulness, gentleness, and self-control in us.

And we know that there is One body, and One Spirit, One hope to which we are called, One Lord, One Faith, One baptism, One God and Father of us all. This is called the unity of the faith that is found in the faith of Jesus Christ.

I do not know of any other bible translation that's primary endeavor is to emphasize and bring to light the faith of the Son of God, which is the one thing that is able to save you from the death and corruption in this present world today unto the hope of the same life you see in the resurrection of Jesus Christ.

Thank you for your interest in The Faith Translation, Thank you for sharing it with your friends and family and for your prayers and support.

Grace and Peace,

John Fazio

PREFACE

A few things you should know and understand about how The Faith Translation is presented.

We understand that through the years and in different cultures and times that words can have various meanings.

We do start with King James language; however, we have changed some of the old KJV language to reflect today's English: Things like, ye to you, whosoever to whoever, shall to will and so on.

The first thing you will notice is the use of parentheses that contain italicized words. These italicized words are the expounding to give understanding to the spirit of what is being said.

With a few exceptions, the words outside of the parentheses are from the Original Greek and those exceptions are italicized as well, but not in parentheses.

Here are two illustrations of each of these.

First, here is an example of italicized words inside parentheses that increase the understanding.

Ephesians 2:15

KJV: 15 Having abolished in his flesh the enmity, even the law of commandments contained in ordinances; for to make in himself of twain one new man, so making peace;

TFT: 15 Having abolished (*the body of death*) in His flesh, (*which death brought*) the hostility (*of our carnal minds toward God's way unto life*), (*and whereby He destroyed*) even (*that which was working death in*) the law of commandments (*through the carnal mind thinking that life was*) contained in (*the keeping of*) ordinances; so that He could in Himself make from the two (*who were both perishing in death*) one new man (*in immortal flesh and bone*), so making peace (*and unity*);

Then, here the words "*your heart*" are italicized words outside of parentheses.

2 Thessalonians 3:3

KJV: 3 But the Lord is faithful, who shall stablish you, and keep *you* from evil.

TFT: 3 But the Lord is faithful, (*being both the One*) who will establish you, (*and who will also strengthen*) and guard *your heart* from evil.

There are some words we have felt to define rather than use, "sin" is one of those words, mostly because of the tendency for many to think that sin is about behavior, when rather sin gets to the root, which is the corrupt wisdom that can animate a man's life and behavior.

Sin is most often a noun that would be defined as: to enlist your members to preserve your own life.

Example 1 Peter 4:1

KJV: 1 Forasmuch then as Christ hath suffered for us in the flesh, arm yourselves likewise with the same mind: for he that hath suffered in the flesh hath ceased from sin;

TFT: 1 Therefore seeing as Christ has suffered for us (*being put to death*) in the flesh, arm yourselves likewise with the same mind: because he who has suffered (*being put to death*) in the flesh (*dies no more and being dead to death*) has ceased from enlisting his members to preserve his own life;

9

At the time of this writing, Galatians to Jude does not contain the word "sin" but it is defined each time in the context which it appears and certainly not ignored.

In another instance in James the word iniquity is used in place of sin.

James 1:15

KJV: 15 Then when lust hath conceived, it bringeth forth sin: and sin, when it is finished, bringeth forth death.

TFT: 15 Then when (*their*) lust (*for life by their own works*) has conceived (*in their heart*), it brings forth (*the sting of death which is*) iniquity: and iniquity, when it is finished, brings forth death.

Righteousness and unrighteousness are two other words that are used but also many times, their meaning is used instead of the word. The reason for this is the same as previously stated regarding sin, that many view these words in regard to behavior, when actually it is simply that God our Father sees it is "unjust" that we were perishing in death, and that is unrighteous or unrighteousness.

The word righteousness is used in quite a few different ways. Each time the context is considered and sometimes it is "justice", sometimes simply "His life" which would be the only life He saw fitting (just) for us from the beginning and that came out of the grave immortal in Jesus.

Here is an example from 1 John, which book I also want to explain seeing as it has no italicized words.

1 John 2:29

KJV: 29 If ye know that he is righteous, ye know that everyone that doeth righteousness is born of him.

TFT: 29 If we know that the One who came from the heart of the Father to testify on our behalf regarding the promise of His life and immortality has been raised up in His incorruptible life, we know that everyone who trusts in Him and His promise of eternal life is born of Him unto the same life.

The book of First John was the first book of The Faith Translation, and it came about so organically, from the Lord, that I did not want to change it. But you will notice its format is a bit different, but still has the same focus to reveal the faith and the testimony of Jesus Christ, which is the spirit of all prophecy.

Lastly, The Faith Translation is best read and understood without pausing at the parentheses ( ) but simply reading through them as part of the sentence. They were added so that should one desire to, they could see and differentiate the exposition from the original Greek.

The Epistle of Paul to the

GALATIANS

The Faith Translation

Chapter 1

1 Paul, an apostle, (*who was*) not sent from men, neither (*did I become an apostle*) through (*the will of*) man, but through Jesus Christ, and God the Father, (*who has called me, revealing His Son in me*) who has raised Him from the dead;

2 And all the brethren (*that fellowship in the truth revealed in Jesus Christ*) which are here with me, (*who can also bear witness*) to all the churches of Ga-la'tia:

3 (*His*) grace and peace be with you from God the Father, and from our Lord Jesus Christ,4 Who gave Himself (*the lamb*) for the death in our flesh, so that He might (*redeem us from the iniquity where we labored in vain through the strength contained in our flesh to preserve our own lives eternally and*) deliver us from this present world that is filled with labors and hardships (*totally free from any spot of death or corruption*) according to the will of God and our Father (*which He has revealed in Christ Jesus our Lord*):

5 To whom (*and from whom*) is all the glory (*for all the ages to come*) forever and ever. Amen.

6 I am amazed that you are so quickly changing from (*trusting in*) Him who has called you by the grace (*and strength*) of Christ unto another gospel (*which is according to your own strength*):

7 Which is not another (*gospel*), but there are some who have stirred up trouble with you who want to pervert the gospel of Christ (*with the wisdom of men*).

8 But even if we or an angel out of heaven should preach a gospel to you contrary to what we declared to you (*publicly setting right before your eyes Christ crucified*), (*their words have already been judged and*) remain to be cursed.

9 As we have said before, even now do I say I again, if anyone preaches any other gospel to you than the one you received (*from us*), (*their words have already been judged and*) remain to be (*that which can only serve you with a*) cursed (*life*).

10 For do (*you think that*) I am suddenly seeking to be persuaded by (*the wisdom of*) men, or God? or do you think I

Galatians 1

seek to (*gain*) the approval of men? Because if I were yet seeking to please men's (*flesh*), I would not be the servant of (*the life of*) Christ (*but the corruption of men*).

11 But I certify to you brethren, that the gospel which was preached (*to you*) by me is not according to the (*corruptible*) wisdom of men (*but from the incorruptible life revealed in Jesus Christ*).

12 Because I neither received (*the gospel*) from man, nor was I taught it (*by any man*), but through the revelation of Jesus Christ.

13 For you have heard about my way of life in times past in Judaism, how that beyond measure I persecuted the church of God and was (*committed to*) destroying it:

14 And I was advancing in Judaism beyond any of my equals in my own nation, seeing as I was more abundantly devoted to the traditions of my fathers (*than any of them were*).

15 But when it pleased God who set me apart from my mother's womb and called me by His grace,

16 To reveal (*the testimony of*) His Son in me (*appearing to me a man in the glory and immortality of God*), so that I might declare Him among the Gentiles (*that justification unto life is found in God and His strength alone and not the strength contained in the flesh*); immediately I did not consult with flesh and blood (*for approval*):

17 Nor did I go up to Jerusalem to (*visit with*) those who were apostles before me: but I went to Arabia and returned again to Damascus (*where I had first encountered the risen Christ*).

18 Then it was not until three years later that I did go to Jerusalem to see Peter and I stayed with him for fifteen days.

19 But of the rest of the apostles I saw none of them except James the Lord's brother.

20 The things which I write to you now, behold, (*I certify*) before God that I lie not.

21 Afterwards I came to the regions of Syr'i-a and Ci-li'cia;

22 And my face was not known to the churches of Judea that were in Christ:

23 But they had only heard that the one which use to persecute us in the past was now preaching the faith (*of Jesus Christ*) which he once destroyed.

24 And they glorified God (*for what He had done*) in me.

Chapter 2

1 Then fourteen years later I went up again to Jerusalem with Barnabas and took Titus with me as well.

2 And I went up (*because of and*) according to the revelation (*which I had received from Christ Jesus Himself*) and set before them (*all*) the gospel which I preached among the Gentiles, but privately (*I went and spoke*) to them who were of reputation (*Peter, James, and John*), (*and they did hear and bore witness in their own hearts the truth of the gospel I preached and*) not that I should be running (*in a different way*) or had run in vain.

3 But not even Titus, who was with me, being a Greek, was compelled (*feeling any obligation*) to be circumcised (*in his flesh to be justified unto life*):

4 And that (*issue only came into question*) because of false brethren (*outside of the faith of Jesus Christ*) who secretly brought in (*strange doctrine*), who came in stealthily to spy out our freedom which we have in Christ Jesus, so that they might bring us into (*the doctrine of*) bondage (*again*):

5 To whom we did not give in to for even a moment so that the truth of the gospel might continue (*to remain and abide*) with you.

6 And regarding those who were esteemed to be (*established Apostles*) with respected opinions, whatever sort they were made no difference to me: For God does not judge a person by outward appearances (*and the opinions of men*): neither did any of those (*apostles*) of reputation lay any new requirement upon me:

7 But on the contrary, when they saw that the gospel to the Gentiles had been entrusted to me (*from the Lord Jesus*), just as the gospel of the circumcision was unto Peter;

Galatians 2

8 Because (*they saw that*) the One that worked in Peter to accomplish the apostleship to the circumcision, is the same (*One*) which was (*working*) mighty in me toward the Gentiles:

9 And when James, Cephas, and John, who were considered to be the pillars, perceived the grace that was given unto me (*from the Lord Jesus*), they extended to me and Barnabas the right hands of fellowship; (*agreeing*) that we should (*continue to*) go to the Gentiles, and they to the circumcision.

10 They only asked that we remember the poor; that which I was also eager to do.

11 However when Peter came to Antioch, I opposed him to his face, because he was to be condemned.

12 Because before certain men arrived with James, he ate with the Gentiles: but once they had come, he withdrew and separated himself from them, fearing (*the opinion*) of them which were of the circumcision (*who think it unlawful to eat with Gentiles*).

13 And the other Jews that were with him also acted hypocritically so that even Barnabas was being led astray by their hypocrisy.

14 But when I saw that they did not conduct themselves straight forward according to the truth of the gospel (*that declared that God has cleansed all flesh from death and has also freely granted the Gentiles justification unto life*), I said to Peter before all of them, if you, being a Jew, live after the manner of Gentiles (*who had not the law*), (*no longer seeking to be justified unto life by performing the deeds of the law*) and not as do the Jews (*who are careful to observe all the deeds of the law*), why do you (*now*) compel the Gentiles to live as do the Jews?

15 We who (*believe in Christ*) are (*inwardly*) Jews by (*partaking of His divine*) nature and are not of those (*who are outwardly Jews but are*) not freely partaking of His life (*but are missing the mark*) like the heathen,

16 Knowing that a man is not justified (*unto immortality in his flesh*) by (*performing*) the deeds of the law, but by the faith of Jesus Christ, even we (*Jews according to the flesh*) have

16

believed in Jesus Christ, so that we might be justified (*from all death's accusations*) by the faith of Christ, and not by (*observing*) the deeds of the law: for by (*performing*) the deeds of the law will no man be justified (*to the immortality of God in their flesh*).

17 But if, while we seek to be justified by Christ, we ourselves are also found to not be freely partaking (*of His life but laboring in our own strength to be justified by performing the deeds and requirements of the law*), does that therefore make Christ the minister of (*the*) death (*that this serves us with*)? Certainly not.

18 For if I (*who once saw in the faith of Jesus Christ that I cannot be justified unto His life and immortality through my flesh*) build up again (*esteeming*) the things which I (*previously saw*) destroyed (*in Christ*), I make myself a transgressor (*of the teaching and instruction of God unto the life in Christ Jesus*).

19 Because I (*being fully persuaded*) by the law (*of the Spirit of life that came out of the grave in the Christ Jesus free from death*) am (*now*) dead to (*death, whereby my carnal mind once held me in the bondage of performing*) the (*deeds of*) law (*in my flesh, so that I might be justified unto His life, which death was truly the very thing that worked in my members to bring forth the fruit of death*), but (*now I am dead to death*) so that I might (*rest in and freely*) live unto God.

20 I am crucified with Christ (*to the corruptible life I can serve myself in the world and the world is crucified to me*): nevertheless (*being dead to death*), I live (*being alive to the life of God*); yet not I (*in my own strength*), but Christ (*who is the wisdom and the power of God*) lives in me (*as my sufficiency to be justified unto His life and immortality in my flesh*): and (*so that*) the life which I now live inside this corruptible body, I live (*being fully persuaded*) by the faith of the Son of God (*by which faith He cried Abba Father*), (*and*) who has demonstrated His great love toward me, giving Himself up for me (*so that He also might raise me up unto His same life and immortality*).

21 I do not make void (*by setting aside*) the grace of God (*revealed in Christ Jesus, to appear in His likeness by His*

strength alone and not my own): because if the life *(and bodily immortality)* of God could come through *(performing the deeds of)* the law, then Christ died in vain.

Chapter 3

1 O *(you)* foolish *(minded)* Galatians, who has cast a spell on you *(that you would no longer reason according to Christ)*, that you would not have confidence in *(and obey)* the truth, before whose very eyes Jesus Christ was *(preached among you and)* openly portrayed as crucified *(being put to death in corruptible flesh but raised unto life in immortal flesh)*?

2 This is the only thing I would like to *(ask and)* hear from you, did you receive the Spirit *(that raised Christ from the dead immortal)* by performing the deeds of the law or by hearing the faith *(of Jesus Christ and Him crucified)*?

3 Are you so foolish *(and void of understanding)* that *(you would reason that)* having begun in the Spirit, you are now *(going to be)* made perfect *(immortal in your flesh)* by *(relying upon)* the *(strength contained in your dying)* flesh?

4 Have you not endured so many things in vain? If you think that *(the promise of the Spirit)* is all for nothing *(believing that you still need to rely upon the strength of your perishable flesh to bring you to perfection)*.

5 The One therefore who supplies the Spirit to you and brings forth miracles among you, is that Spirit *(which comes from Him to you)* born in you by your ability to perform the deeds of the law or by the hearing of the faith *(of Jesus Christ)*?

6 Even Abraham *(has heard and)* believed *(upon the One)* God *(promised He would send, and he rejoiced to see His day)* and the same life *(and immortality)* which comes through *(the)* faith *(of Jesus Christ)* was concluded by him *(revealed)* to be the way which he would inherit the life of God *(and become the father of many nations)*.

7 Therefore we know then that they which are born from the faith *(of Jesus Christ)*, the same are the descendants of Abraham *(in the faith)*.

8 And the scripture, foreseeing that God would (*also freely*) justify the heathen (*unto His life*) through faith, foretold the gospel to Abraham, saying, in you (*and your seed*) shall all nations be blessed (*by believing upon the same faith*).

9 So then they which are born from (*hearing and believing upon the*) faith (*of Jesus Christ*) are blessed with (*the same life and immortality*) along with faithful Abraham.

10 But as many as rely upon (*the strength of their own hands*) to perform the deeds of the law (*to be justified to that same life*) are under the curse (*the way which will only serve them with death*): because it is written, cursed is every one that does not continue (*to believe*) in all the things which are written in the book of the law to obey them (*which obedience, was never found in their ability to perform carnal commandments but rather in trust toward God*).

11 And we know that no man is justified unto the life (*and immortality of God*) by his own strength and ability to perform the deeds of the law in the sight of God, it is (*clearly*) evident (*and manifested in the faith of Jesus Christ*), that the (*one*) justified unto that life will live by (*obeying the same*) faith (*revealed in Jesus Christ*).

12 And (*relying upon performing carnal commandments of*) the law (*to be justified unto life and immortality in your flesh*) is not born from the faith (*of Jesus Christ*) but the man who wants to be judged (*and justified*) by them (*is bound*) to live in (*the judgments of*) them (*and the fruit of death that worshipping the works of their own hands brings forth*).

13 Christ has redeemed us from the curse (*of death, which caused us to labor in our carnal minds to be justified unto blessing and life by performing the deeds of the law, which is*) the curse of (*death that used*) the law (*of carnal commandments to work the fruit of death in us*), (*but Christ*) has become a curse for us (*taking our death upon Himself*): because it is written, cursed (*by death*) is every one that hangs on a tree:

14 So that the (*same*) blessing (*and life promised*) to Abraham (*and his seed*) might come also on the Gentiles through (*the*

Galatians 3

faith) of Jesus Christ; so that we all (*Jew or Gentile*) might receive the promise of the Spirit (*being persuaded*) by the faith (*revealed in Jesus Christ*).

15 Brethren, I speak as a man: As though it were only a man's covenant, but (*even with a man's covenant*) once it has been ratified, no man can (*ignore*), do away with, or add (*anything*) to it.

16 Now to Abraham and his seed (*did God*) make the promises. He does not say to seeds as if its many, but as of one (*seed*), and to your seed which is Christ.

17 And furthermore I say this, that the covenant which was confirmed (*beforehand*) by God in Christ, the law, which came four hundred and thirty years later, can in no way cancel (*or add to the promise*), that it could (*in anyway*) make the promise of (*eternal life of*) no effect.

18 Truly therefore if the inheritance (*of eternal life*) comes from (*the deeds of*) the law, it is no longer by promise: but God gave it to Abraham (*and his seed*) by promise.

19 For what purpose then did the law serve? It was added (*not as an addition to the promise but*) because of the transgressions of Israel when they were led out of Egypt by the strength of God's hand (*so that they might know that trusting in the works of their own hands for life was biting them with the serpents death, and so that their eyes would be kept on Gods promise to serve them with life*) until (*Christ*), the seed to whom the promise was made should come (*to fulfill it*); and because Moses could not see God's face and live it was given to him by the hands of the angels.

20 Now (*with man*) a mediator is not a mediator of one (*but between two parties*) but God is One (*the only immortal, and since He is the only One who could promise, so also is He the only One who was able to perform it in Christ*).

21 Is the law therefore against the promises of God (*to give you His blessing and life as a gift*)? May it never be said: For if there had been a law which was able to (*conquer death and*) impart (*eternal*) life (*and immortality in the flesh*), then the

(*only*) life (*which God saw fitting for all men from the beginning*) could have come by the law.

22 But (*the law being only a shadow and not the substance was not opposed to the promises but rather impotent in its ability to conquer death in the flesh and*) the scripture had concluded that all were dead (*laboring in bondage to be justified in their dying flesh*), so that the promise (*of eternal life, the substance of*) which came by the faith revealed in Jesus Christ (*being raised from the grave in immortal flesh*) might be freely given to them that believe.

23 But before (*the substance of*) faith came (*in Jesus Christ*), we were kept under (*the schoolmaster of*) the law, shut in together (*unto our eyes being fixed on the faith*) until the faith that would afterwards be revealed (*would come in the death, burial, bodily resurrection, and ascension of Jesus Christ*).

24 Wherefore the law was our tutor (*chastising the way we formerly thought was unto life, showing us that trusting in the strength of our own hands only served us with the fruit of death and*) leading us to Christ, so that we might be justified (*to the life and immortality of God as sons*) through the faith (*revealed in Jesus Christ*).

25 But after the faith is come (*in Christ*), we are no longer under a schoolmaster (*having received the promise made immortal flesh*).

26 For you are all (*declared to be*) the sons of God by the faith (*revealed*) in Christ Jesus (*our Lord*).

27 For as many of you as have been baptized into Christ' (*death and resurrection*) have put on (*the same life of a son revealed in*) Christ.

28 There is no longer Jew or Greek, there is no longer bond or free, there is not male or female: for you are all one in Christ Jesus (*our Lord*).

29 And if you be Christ's, then you are Abraham's seed, and heirs (*of God*) according to the promise (*of eternal life revealed in Christ Jesus*).

Chapter 4

1 Now I say this, that the heir, as long as he is still a child, is no different from a servant, though he is the lord of all;

2 But remains under tutors and governors until the time appointed by the father.

3 Even so we (*the heirs of God*), when we were children, were in bondage, under the elements of the world (*with all its death and corruption*):

4 But when the fulness of the time was come, God sent forth His Son, (*His incorruptible seed being*) born from a woman, born (*a man*) under the law (*subject to all the same elements in the world*),

5 To redeem those (*from death and corruption*) who were under the law (*and in bondage to the elements of the world*), so that we might (*freely*) receive all the fullness (*of His life and immortality*) as (*His*) sons.

6 And because you are (*His*) sons, God has sent forth the Spirit of His Son into your hearts, crying, Abba, Father.

7 Therefore you are no longer a servant (*in bondage to death and corruption*), but a (*full grown*) son; and if you are a son, then you are an inheritor of (*the life of*) God (*which was revealed*) in (*the resurrection of*) Jesus Christ (*His Son*).

8 Why is it then that when you (*were under death's reign and*) did not know God (*as Father*), you performed service to them which by nature are not gods at all (*possessing no ability to serve you with life but only death*).

9 But now, after that you have known God (*as Father*), or rather are known (*as the sons*) of God, why (*would you*) turn again to these weak and destitute elements (*contained in the world of touch not, taste not, handle not*), do you desire to be in bondage again (*to their death and corruption*)?

10 You observe days, and months, and times, and years.

11 I am afraid (*and marvel*) concerning your (*reasoning*), that perhaps all the labor I was compelled to give to you has been in vain.

12 Brethren, I implore you, to be (*free from bondage*) as I am; for I have become as you (*Gentiles*) are, and you have not done any wrong to me.

13 You know how that in the weakness of my flesh I proclaimed the gospel to you at first.

14 And the temptation (*to disregard me which came to you*) because of the weakness of my flesh you did not despise, neither did you reject me; but you received me like an angel of God, even like Christ Jesus (*Himself*).

15 What then has (*become of*) that joy of yours? for I bear record of you, that, if it had been possible, you would have plucked out your own eyes, and have given them to me.

16 So, have I now become your enemy, because I tell you the truth?

17 They (*who came to you of the circumcision*) are jealous of you, but not in a good way (*according to the truth in Christ*); but rather they desire to exclude you, so that you might be jealous of them.

18 But it is always a good thing to be desirous of the truth (*according to the knowledge of Christ*), and not only when I am present with you.

19 My little children, of whom I am again travailing in birth until Christ be (*completely*) formed in you,

20 I desire to be present with you now (*face to face*), and to change my (*tone of*) voice (*so that you do not think I am your enemy*); for I am perplexed by you (*that you have been so soon removed from the gospel of Christ that I proclaimed*).

21 Tell me, (*those of*) you who desire to be subject to (*the bondage and curse that comes from laboring to be justified unto life and immortality in the weakness of your flesh, by performing all the outward ordinances of*) the law, do you not hear (*the spirit of*) the law (*written in the scriptures*)?

22 For it is written, that Abraham had two sons, the one born from a bondwoman, the other by a freewoman.

23 But he who was (*born*) of the bondwoman was born after (*the will of*) the flesh; but he that was (*born*) of the freewoman was by (*the Spirit of*) promise (*God gave to Abraham*).

23

Galatians 5

24 Which things are (*to be understood as*) an allegory: for these are two covenants; the one from mount Sinai, the one (*after the flesh*) which gives birth to bondage, which is Agar.

25 For this Agar is mount Sinai in Arabia and corresponds to (*natural*) Jerusalem that exists now, and which (*being born of the flesh*) is in bondage (*and along*) with her children (*desolate*).

26 But (*the heavenly*) Jerusalem which is (*from*) above is the free woman (*born from the Spirit of promise*), which (*Spirit*) is the mother of us all.

27 For it is written, Rejoice, you (*who were*) barren, that did not bear (*because I refused your union to death, says the Lord*); break forth and cry (*for joy, forgetting the shame of your youth*), you that did not travail: because many are the children born desolate (*from the flesh*) but (*the children born from the promise of the Spirit*) are those who see (*their maker is their*) husband (*who are barren no more because of the promised seed*).

28 Now we (*who are born of the Spirit*), brethren, are as Isaac was, the children (*born*) from the promise (*of the Spirit*).

29 But just like then, he that was born after the flesh persecuted him that was born after the Spirit, even so is it now.

30 But what does the scripture say? Cast out the bondwoman and her son: because the son of the bondwoman will by no means receive an inheritance (*along*) with the (*rightful*) son of the freewoman.

31 So then, brethren, we are not servants born from the bondwoman (*after the flesh*), but of the free (*the sons of God, born from the Spirit*).

Chapter 5

1 It is for freedom that Christ has set us free (*from death, which formerly had us laboring in our flesh to obtain to life*), stand firm therefore in the liberty (*the Father has given you in Christ*) and do not become entangled again with (*the weight of*) this doctrine (*that came*) from (*the*) bondage (*of death*).

2 Listen carefully, I Paul, say to you, that if (*you are seeking to be justified to life and immortality in the flesh, through the strength of your dying flesh*) being circumcised (*in your flesh*), Christ, (*who has circumcised you from that body of death*), will profit you nothing.

3 For I testify again to every man that is circumcised (*relying upon the strength of their corruptible flesh, to observe all the deeds of the law*), that he is (*under a curse*) a debtor (*in bondage*) to do the whole law.

4 You have rendered (*the strength of God in*) Christ (*to freely justify you unto life and immortality by the Spirit*) of no effect, whosoever of you are (*relying upon your own strength to be*) justified (*to immortality in the flesh*) by (*observing*) the (*deeds of the*) law; you are fallen (*away*) from grace (*if you cease from trusting in the strength of God alone to freely justify you unto His life*).

5 For we (*who rely upon the strength of God in Christ to justify us*) by the Spirit, eagerly await the (*sure*) hope of the life (*and immortality of God*) through the faith (*that was revealed in Jesus Christ*).

6 Because in Christ Jesus neither does (*trusting in*) being circumcised, or uncircumcised, contain any power (*to raise you up to His life and immortality*); but (*only the hearing of*) faith which works (*in your heart to persuade you*) of His love (*to freely justify you by His Spirit unto that life*).

7 You were running well; who has hindered you that you should not obey the truth (*which has been so clearly set before you in Christ and Him crucified*)?

8 This persuasion does not come from Him who calls you (*from out of the darkness that death brought, into the liberty of His incorruptible life*).

9 A little leaven leavens the whole lump (*as a little corruption, corrupts the whole*).

10 I have confidence in you, that through the Lord, you will not be of any other mind (*than His*): but he that troubles you will bear His judgment (*concerning what that corrupt persuasion will serve them with*), whoever that may be.

Galatians 5

11 And I, my brothers (*in Christ*), if I still preach circumcision (*as some suggest*), why do I still suffer persecution (*from my circumcised brethren according to the flesh*)? If that were the case, the offense which comes from the cross (*of Christ to those who boast in their flesh would have*) ceased.

12 I wish that those who have upset you would (*not only circumcise themselves but*) were even (*totally*) cut off (*castrating themselves*).

13 For, brethren, you have been called unto freedom (*delivered from the bondage of death, to the glorious liberty of His life*); see that you do not (*return to bondage*) by using your freedom as an occasion to (*boast in*) the (*strength of your corruptible*) flesh, but rather (*abide*) in (*the*) love (*which He has served you with in freeing you from death*) serving one another (*in that love*).

14 For the entire law is fulfilled (*in Christ*) in one word, (*love*), (*abiding in Him*) inside of this (*love by which He has loved us*); You will love (*and prefer*) your neighbor's (*life*) as your own.

15 But if you bite and devour one another, (*beware*) that you are not (*completely*) consumed by one another.

16 This I say then, walk, (*resting*) in the (*sure promise of the*) Spirit (*to justify you unto life and immortality in your flesh*), and you will not fulfill the lust (*to bring forth life*) from the flesh.

17 Because the lusts contained in the flesh (*to serve itself with life*) are opposed to (*the way of*) the Spirit of God (*to freely serve you with His life*), and the Spirit opposed to (*the way of*) the flesh: and these (*two*) are contrary, the one to the other (*one leading to death and the other to life*): so that you cannot (*through the lust of the flesh*) bring forth the things that your heart (*truly*) desires.

18 But if you are led by the Spirit (*of life that is in Christ Jesus, which raised Him up from the dead, to freely serve you with that same life and immortality in your flesh*), you, being freed from (*the bondage of death*) are no longer under the law (*where that body of death brought you into captivity, laboring to serve yourself with life through your dying flesh*).

19 Now the works that are manifest (*from trusting in the strength*) of the flesh (*to father your life*) are these; fornication (*being intimate with the works of your hands*), uncleanness (*a mind filled with and defiled by death*), lasciviousness (*an unrestrained lust for the life you can gather to yourself*),

20 Idolatry, (*rejecting the true God, to worship other gods made with man's hands which is*) witchcraft (*born from rebellion*), hatred (*and hostility*), strife (*an affection to argue and dispute all things*), jealousies, outbursts of anger, contentions (*and selfish rivalries*), dissensions (*which cause division*) heresies (*separating themselves as chosen or possessing special knowledge*),

21 Filled with envy, (*spite and ill will*), excessive intoxication, and riotous living, and things like these: of which I tell you now, beforehand, just as I have also told you in the past, that those who do these things (*to father their own lives with the life they can get from the world*) will not possess (*or experience*) the life (*of a son*) of God, (*having set aside His grace, wherein He desires to freely serve them with the same life as His beloved Son by the Spirit*).

22 But the fruit (*that comes from trusting in God to Father your life*) from the Spirit is love, joy, peace, long-suffering, gentleness, goodness, faith,

23 Meekness, self-control: there is no law (*that can bring accusation*) against such things (*for those who wait, trusting upon the Spirit of God to freely serve them with these things are blameless according to the law*).

24 And they that are Christ's have crucified the flesh (*along*) with the affections and lusts (*of its members, resting in the sure hope of His life and immortality in the flesh, revealed in the faith of Jesus Christ*).

25 If (*the life*) we live (*in the flesh, we live by the faith of the Son of God, to serve us with His life*) by the Spirit, let us also walk by the (*same*) Spirit (*so that His life would be fulfilled in us who walk not after the flesh but after the Spirit*).

26 Let us not become boastful (*in the strength we can obtain to*) in our flesh (*which glorying is void of any power to inherit*

His life), (*but that which only*) provokes us to challenge one another, (*causing us to*) envy (*where we bite and devour*) one another.

Chapter 6

1 Brethren, (*even*) should a man be overcome in some fault (*which ensnares him in an error*), you who (*are led by and*) walk after the Spirit, (*are able to*) restore such a man with the fruit of gentleness (*which the Spirit gives*); considering yourself (*and the weakness of your own flesh*), so that you will not also be tempted (*to glory in the flesh but in the Spirit*).

2 Remove the weight (*that death brings to the heart*) from each other's burdens (*by declaring how Christ Jesus has conquered our death in the flesh*) and in doing so (*you will*) fulfill the teaching and instruction of Christ (*unto life*).

3 Because if a man thinks that within himself (*that is, in his own heart*) that he can (*produce*) something (*good in his corruptible flesh*), when he has no good thing in his flesh (*that can produce anything but death*), he deceives himself.

4 But let each man discern, (*what serves with life and what serves with death*) in his own heart (*by Christ Jesus*) and then will his glorying be (*in Christ*) within his heart alone and not in another (*man's persuasion*).

5 Because every man will bear the weight of his own burden (*whether he is trusting in the flesh unto corruption or of the Spirit unto eternal life*).

6 Moreover, let the one who is being taught in the word (*of eternal life*) share (*in the same fellowship along*) with him that teaches in all good things.

7 Do not be deceived; You cannot mock (*or ignore the word and judgment of*) God (*in Christ*): for whatever (*word*) is planted (*and has taken root*) in a man's (*heart*), from that (*word he is trusting upon*) will he also reap (*its fruit*).

8 For he that trusts in (*the strength of*) his flesh will of the flesh reap corruption; but he that trusts upon the Spirit will of the Spirit reap life everlasting (*even unto immortality in his flesh*).

9 And let us (*who trust upon the Spirit*) not exhaust ourselves in working (*the*) good (*which we can bring forth*): because at the opportune time we (*by the Spirit*) will reap (*the good fruit of His life*), if we (*rest in Him and*) not faint (*in our own exhaustion*).

10 So then, as we (*by the Spirit*) have opportunity, let us be workers of the good (*which the Spirit brings forth*) toward all (*men*), especially to those who (*along with you*) are devoted to the faith (*of Jesus Christ*).

11 Notice how (*that with*) large letters I, (*Paul*) have written to you by my own hand.

12 As many as desire to make a good show (*by glorying in their outward appearance*) in their flesh, they compel you (*also*) to be circumcised, in order that they might not suffer persecution (*from their circumcised brethren*) for (*the offense that comes from*) the cross of Christ (*to those who boast in their flesh*).

13 Because not even those who are circumcised keep the law; but they (*only*) desire to have you circumcised, so that in your flesh they may glory (*in that you have submitted to their way, lording over you in it*).

14 But as for me, may it never be that I should glory, (*boasting*) in anything other than in the cross of our Lord Jesus Christ, by whom the world is crucified to me, and I to the world.

15 Because in (*the death and resurrection of*) Christ Jesus (*we see that*) neither being circumcised nor uncircumcised is anything (*that could ever serve us with immortality in our dying flesh*) but only a new creature (*that is forever free of death and corruption*).

16 And as many as walk with this (*faith revealed in the Lord Jesus*) as their guide, will have peace (*and rest in their flesh*) and (*the Father's*) mercy (*to remove their suffering at the hands of death resting upon them*), and upon (*all who place their trust in Him*) the (*true*) Israel of God.

17 From now on, let no man bother me (*regarding the mark of circumcision*): Because I carry in my body the marks (*which I received for the testimony*) of the Lord Jesus.

Galatians 6

18 Brethren, the grace (*and peace*) of our Lord Jesus Christ be with your spirit. Amen.

The Epistle of Paul to the

EPHESIANS

The Faith Translation

Chapter 1

1 Paul, an apostle (*and messenger of the gospel*) of Jesus Christ by the will of God, to all those set apart for His life that are in Ephesus, and to ones who are persuaded by the faith of Christ Jesus:

2 (*His*) grace and (*the*) peace (*it gives*) to you from God the Father and from our Lord Jesus Christ (*be with you all*).

3 Spoken well of and highly celebrated with the most eloquent of speech is the God and Father of our Lord Jesus Christ, who has bestowed upon us (*His children*) the same blessing, in the word He spoke about us in Christ Jesus who is seated (*an immortal man in the glory and honor of the Father*) at the right hand of Majesty on high.

4 Exactly as He has chosen us (*to be*) in Him before (*death entered at*) the foundation of the world, so that we would be set apart (*for His life*) and (*stand*) without accusation before Him in love:

5 Having determined (*from the beginning*) that we (*as His children*) should have His (*same*) life, has He now declared us as His rightful children and sons through (*the resurrection of the man*) Jesus Christ (*redeeming us back*) to Himself (*and His original purpose for us*), and according to the good pleasure (*and satisfaction*) of His will,

6 To the (*only life that He determined was*) praiseworthy (*and fitting for His children*) of His good view (*and opinion which He declared*) in His grace (*toward them in raising Jesus Christ to His life and immortality*), wherein He has also (*loved us and*) freely given us the same life (*preserving our lives incorruptible inside of the*) Beloved.

7 In whom we have redemption (*from death*) through His blood (*that ran out, releasing us from death's bondage*), the sending away of (*its sting*) our trespasses (*wherein we formerly labored in vain*), showing forth the riches of His grace (*kindness and mercy towards us through Christ Jesus*);

8 Wherein He has lavished upon us (*His love and has given us*) all wisdom and understanding;

32

9 Having made known (*by openly unveiling*) to us the mystery of His will (*towards us all*), according to His good pleasure which He has purposed in Himself (*from the before world began*):

10 And (*having purposed it*) does He (*also*) oversee it (*to completion, so that*) in the fullness of time, He might gather together all things as one in Christ, (*so that*) both that which is in heaven and on the earth would be joined as one (*incorruptible*) in Him.

11 In (*Him*) whom also we have obtained an (*eternal*) inheritance (*of His life and immortality*), which (*life*) He predetermined (*for us His children from the beginning*) according to the purpose of the One (*God and Father*) who works all things after the (*plan and*) counsel of His own will:

12 So that we should be (*One with His life*), the (*only life which He*) approved (*and saw fitting*) for (*His children*) of His glory, (*in us*) who first hoped (*looking for the life that*) Christ (*would bring*).

13 In whom (*also*) you (*have*) trusted (*and hoped*), after that you heard the word of truth (*for all people*), the gospel of your salvation (*from death and corruption*): in whom after you believed has He set the seal (*of His sonship*) upon you (*marking you*) with that Holy Spirit (*by which He has*) promised (*us His life*),

14 Which (*Spirit*) is the guarantee of the inheritance (*of Christ*) until the redemption of our (*corruptible*) bodies (*immortal*) unto the (*only life which He*) approved (*and saw fitting*) for (*His children*) of His glory.

15 Because of this have I also after hearing of the faith that you have among you in the Lord Jesus and the love you have for all those who are sharing (*with you*) in His life,

16 Have not ceased to give thanks for you, making mention of you in my prayers;

17 That the God (*and Father*) of our Lord Jesus Christ, The Father of glory, may give to you the spirit of wisdom and revelation (*that is contained within Christ*) the knowledge of Him:

Ephesians 2

18 (*So that*) the eyes of your understanding would be illuminated (*to see clearly*); so that you may (*intimately*) know (*Him*) and the (*sure*) hope (*of the life He has promised in Christ*) that He has (*desired*), invited (*and prepared*) for you (*from the beginning*), and what are the riches that come from His glory (*which is*) His inheritance in all those who desire to share in His life,

19 And (*that you may know*) what is the surpassing greatness of His strength (*and ability*) in us who are persuaded (*trusting that He will bring forth His life in us*), by the (*same*) operation of His mighty power,

20 Which He has openly demonstrated in Christ, when He raised Him from the dead (*a man in immortal flesh and bone never to die again*), and set Him at His own right hand in heavenly places,

21 (*A place*) far above all wisdom, (*knowledge*) and power, and strength, and authority, and every name that can be named, not only in this world, but also in the world which is to come:

22 And has put all things under His feet, and has given (*Himself*) in Jesus Christ (*the beginning of the creation of God, the first born from the dead*) to be the head over all wisdom to the church,

23 Which is His body, (*wherein all*) the fullness (*dwells*) from the One who fills all in all.

Chapter 2

1 And you (*has He restored to life*) who were dead from the transgression (*that left you dead and*) laboring in the weakness of your corruptible flesh (*by the sweat of your brow*) to establish your own life (*which always fell short of the mark of eternal life that could bring immortality to your flesh which God desired to give you as a gift*).

2 And in (*this offense*) did you walk (*out of the way*) in times past according to the spirit contained in the world, by the deadly principles of (*the serpent*) the ruling influence of the world by which corruption entered therein, the spirit (*that is opposed to Christ*) which (*even*) now works in the (*hearts of*

the) children who refuse to be persuaded (*by the faith of Jesus Christ*).

3 Among whom in times past we also were all children conducting our lives in the same manner in the lust (*to bring forth life through the strength contained*) in our flesh, laboring in all the things our flesh desired (*and thought would bring life and peace*) from every imagination of the carnal mind; and which were by origin the very things (*that bring death*) which God has sworn in His passion (*for us*) to destroy, which things were fathering our lives, (*as children who were walking out of the way*) even as others.

4 But God, who is rich (*and abundant*) in mercy (*and everlasting kindness toward us*), and because of His great love by which He loved us (*desiring to preserve our lives forever with Him*),

5 (*So that*) even when we were dead and in bondage, laboring in vain to preserve our lives in (*the weakness of*) our corruptible flesh, has He made us alive together with Christ, by His grace and strength (*and not our own*) you are saved (*from death*);

6 And He has raised us up together and seated us together in heavenly places in Christ Jesus:

7 In order that in the ages to come He might show us the exceeding riches of His grace (*the blessing and life*) which He has bestowed upon us (*surpassing all that we could ask, think, or imagine*) in His (*everlasting*) kindness toward us through Christ Jesus.

8 Because by (*His*) grace (*and strength*) are you saved (*from death*) through (*being persuaded of the*) faith (*that was made flesh in Jesus Christ, which faith is full of power to animate you with His life*); and it is not (*something you can bring forth*) in yourself, but it is the gift of God:

9 Not as a result of (*my own*) works, lest any man should boast (*in his ability and not God's*).

10 Because we are His workmanship, which He created (*through the Spirit of faith to form us in the image*) of Christ Jesus (*and established*) upon (*the*) good works (*that He has

done), which (*works*) He has before ordained (*from the beginning, before death entered*) that we should walk in His good works (*and the fruit of His life*).

11 Therefore remember that in times past you who are Gentiles according to the flesh were called uncircumcised (*and unclean*) by those who were circumcised in their (*corruptible*) flesh by (*man's*) hands;

12 And at that time you were without Christ, and aliens with no citizenship in Israel, and estranged (*without knowledge or share in*) the covenants of promise, having no hope, and without God (*believing you were orphans*) in the world:

13 But now in Christ Jesus you who at one time were far off are made near by the blood (*that ran out*) of Christ.

14 Because He Himself is the (*one that brought*) unity (*and has made peace between Jew and Gentile in conquering the death that reigned over them*), whereby He made both (*those who were near and those who were far*) one (*new man*), and has broken down the middle wall of separation that was between us contained in the (*confidence of corruptible*) flesh;

15 Having abolished (*the body of death*) in His flesh, (*which death brought*) the hostility (*of our carnal minds toward God's way unto life*), (*and whereby He destroyed*) even (*that which was working death in*) the law of commandments (*through the carnal mind thinking that life was*) contained in (*the keeping of*) ordinances; so that He could in Himself make from the two (*who were both perishing in death*) one new man (*in immortal flesh and bone*), so making peace (*and unity*);

16 So that He might join us both back together unto Himself in (*the unity of*) one body (*flesh of His flesh and bone of His bone*) through the cross, having destroyed death (*in the flesh*), and the hostility thereby:

17 And (*now has He*) come preaching that peace (*found in the unity of the faith*) to both you who were far off and to them that were near.

18 Because through Him (*this one new man*) do we both have access by one (*and the same*) Spirit (*which raised Him from the*

dead) and has joined us both in the union (*of one body*) to the Father.

19 Now therefore you are no longer strangers and foreigners, but fellow citizens with those sharing in His life and you are from the household of God (*His workmanship*);

20 And built upon the (*one and only*) foundation of (*which*) the apostles and prophets (*spoke*), Jesus Christ Himself who is the chief corner stone (*and the head of all wisdom to the body*);

21 In (*Christ*) whom the entire body (*the church dwells*) perfectly joined together (*in Him*) into an ever-increasing temple (*not made with man's hands*) the place which He set apart for you (*to dwell*) in the Lord:

22 In whom you also are built together (*and set apart*) for a dwelling of God through the Spirit.

Chapter 3

1 For this reason I Paul, the prisoner (*held captive and compelled by the love*) of Jesus Christ for you Gentiles,

2 If you have indeed been listening (*carefully to the unfolding mystery and*) to the stewardship of the grace of God which has been entrusted to me to give to you:

3 How that by revelation (*of Jesus Christ*) He made known to me the mystery (*that was from before the world began*); just as I have written before in few words,

4 So that when you read them, you may understand my knowledge (*which is contained and revealed*) in the mystery of Christ.

5 Which in previous times was not made known to the sons of men, as it is now revealed to His holy apostles and prophets through the Spirit;

6 (*Revealing*) that the Gentiles (*along with the Jews*) should be co-inheritors, and of the same body, and partakers of His (*same*) promise in Christ through the gospel:

7 And it is of (*this gospel*) which I (*Paul*) have been made a (*servant and effective*) minister, according to the gift of the

Ephesians 3

grace of God given to me (*by revelation of Jesus Christ*) through the working of His power.

8 In me, who (*according to my persecution of the church*) am less than the least of all the saints, is this (*same*) grace (*and ability*) given me, that I should declare among the Gentiles the immeasurable riches of Christ;

9 And to make it plain for all men to see (*revealing*) how God has unfolded and administered (*the fellowship*) of this mystery, which from the beginning of the world (*until now*) has been hid in God, who created all things by Jesus Christ:

10 So that now to the rulers and authorities in heavenly places (*it should be made known*) through the body (*of the risen Christ*) the innumerable and precious intricacies of the wisdom of God,

11 According to the eternal purpose which He purposed (*from the beginning*) in Christ Jesus our Lord:

12 In whom we have boldness and access (*to approach Him*) with confidence (*of reward being persuaded by*) the faith of Jesus Christ.

13 Therefore my desire is that you do not become discouraged at my affliction (*which I have suffered*) for (*preaching the gospel to*) you, which (*speaks*) your glory (*and brings great consolation and salvation*).

14 For this reason I bend my knees (*to pray*) to the Father of our Lord Jesus Christ,

15 From whom every family in heaven and earth is surnamed,

16 (*Asking*) that He would give to you, according to (*the exceeding*) riches of His glory (*and good opinion of you*), to be strengthened with (*His glorious*) power by His Spirit in the inner man;

17 So that (*the Spirit and wisdom of*) Christ may (*be settled in you*) dwelling (*permanently*) in your hearts by faith (*ever*) persuading (*you of His life and union to you*); so that being firmly planted, (*rooted and*) established in His love,

18 That you would be able to (*fully*) comprehend (*and lay hold of along*) with all the saints what is (*the magnitude of*) the

width and the length and the depth, and the height (*of His love for you*);

19 And to know (*and fellowship with*) the love of Christ, which (*intimacy*) surpasses (*all*) knowledge, so that you might be filled (*and complete*) with all the fullness of God (*Himself*).

20 And unto Him who is able (*and desires*) to do (*far beyond*) exceeding (*all that our hearts ever hoped for*) super abundantly above all that we could ask or think (*or imagine*), through His power (*and might alone*) which (*He*) works in us,

21 To Him (*and from Him is*) all the glory in the church by Christ Jesus throughout all the ages (*to come*), (*and for all eternity in the new heaven and new earth*) a world that has no end. Amen.

Chapter 4

1 Therefore do I Paul, the prisoner (*captivated and compelled by the love*) of Jesus Christ (*for all people*) implore you to walk (*as children of the light*) in a manner fitting of the same life (*that was in Him who bears the life*) for which you are (*also*) called,

2 With all lowliness of heart (*thinking nothing of your ability to bring forth that life*) and in meekness (*not attempting to establish it by your own works but trusting the Father to give it to you as a gift*) with much patience, bearing with one another in love;

3 Being diligent to observe the unity (*of the faith*), the Spirit (*that*) bonds us as one.

4 One body and one Spirit, even the one hope of the life (*and immortality*) which He has called you all to;

5 One Lord, one faith, one baptism,

6 One God and Father of all, who is above all and through all, and in you all.

7 But to every one of us (*has He*) given (*the gift of*) the grace (*of God*) the full measure of which is (*in the body of*) Christ Jesus (*seated in immortal flesh and bone at His right hand*).

Ephesians 4

8 This is why (*the Psalmist*) says, when He ascended up (*to the right hand of majesty on*) high that He led those held captive under deaths reign from their captivity and (*having received from the Father*) He gave gifts to men (*so that He might dwell with them*).

9 Now (*if we know*) that He ascended up, what (*good*) is it (*for us*) if He did not also descend first into (*the grave in*) the lower parts of the earth?

10 (*But thanks be to God we know that*) He who descended (*into the grave*) is the same One who also ascended up (*being exalted by the Father*) far above all the heavens, so that He might fulfill (*and bring*) all things (*to completion in one body*).

11 And He has given some (*members of the body the gift to be*), apostles; and some, prophets; and some, evangelists; and some, pastors, and teachers (*who all speak the same truth contained in Christ*);

12 (*Which parts of the body work together*) to completely furnish the saints, for the work of ministering (*the faith of Christ and*) for the building up of the body of Christ:

13 Until we all come in the unity of the faith (*of Jesus Christ*), and (*to the peace*) that comes from the knowledge of the Son of God; to (*the certainty of the same life in Him*) a perfect man, (*according*) to the measure of the life (*which God has purposed for us from the beginning*) the fulness of (*which is in*) Christ:

14 So that we would no longer be like immature children that are tossed back and forth by the waves and carried away by every wind of empty (*and useless*) teachings which come by the trickery of men and the cunning cleverness, which schemes are always there waiting in an attempt to deceive you;

15 But rather, (*by*) speaking the truth (*contained in Christ*) in love, may we (*be established in the faith*) growing into the fullness (*of Him*) in all things, who is the head (*cornerstone of all wisdom and knowledge to the body*), even Christ:

16 From whom the entire body is perfectly joined and held together and by which every ligament is nourished and supplied; according to (*Him*) effectually working in every part,

to make the (*entire*) body increase (*being*) built up (*and established*) in (*His*) love.

17 This I say therefore, and declare by the testimony of the Lord, that you should no longer walk as Gentiles (*previously*) walked (*having no hope without God in the world*), in the futility of their (*own*) mind (*devoid of the truth*),

18 Having their understanding darkened (*by the death in the world*), being alienated from (*the promise of*) the life of God through the ignorance that is in (*their carnal*) minds, because of the (*death which brought*) blindness to their heart:

19 Who having become callous (*to their own despair*) have given themselves over to an unbridled lust (*for the life they can serve themselves*), to work everything that is unclean (*touching the death and corruption in the world*) and never able to satisfy their desire for more.

20 But you have not learned this from (*the faith of*) Jesus Christ;

21 If in fact you have truly heard Him, and have been taught by Him, according to the truth which is (*only found*) in Jesus:

22 So that you (*might*) lay down (*the burden of establishing your own life*) regarding the way you formerly conducted your life, the old man (*who was dead and laboring for life*), which (*way*) is corrupt according to the deceitful lust (*for life from things that cannot ever give you the life your heart truly desires but which can only serve you with death and corruption*);

23 And (*so that you would*) be renewed in the spirit of your mind (*by beholding the faith and considering the new man that emerged from the grave immortal, Christ Jesus*):

24 And that you would be clothed by (*the life of*) the new man, who after the likeness of God is created (*through the Spirit of faith*) incorruptible (*free from death and corruption, in the same life and immortality you see in Christ Jesus*), the true (*life*) which He has set apart for you (*from the beginning*).

25 For this reason lay aside the lies (*which caused you to try and establish your own life*) and speak the truth (*revealed in the faith of Jesus Christ*) to everyone of your neighbors: because we are all members of one another (*in Him*).

Ephesians 5

26 Stand in awe of Him (*and His ability to give you His life*), and (*you will*) cease from all your labor: do not allow your passion for life as an occasion to do evil (*which is to establish your own life*) but stand still (*in awe of Him*):

27 And (*where you*) do not give an opportunity for the accusation which originates from the devil (*that you are not His son or daughter filled with glory and honor from the Father*).

28 Let him who (*from the lack which death served him with*) stole, steal no more (*seeing that he has all things in Christ*): but rather let him use his energy working with his hands the thing which is good (*while resting in God's sufficiency*), so that he may give (*from a heart filled with abundance*) to him that has need.

29 Let no corrupt (*and useless*) communication (*that has no ability to give life*) come out of your mouth, but (*only*) that which is good (*and perfect and has come down from the Father, who is the only giver of life*) to the use of building (*one up in the faith of Jesus Christ*), so that the hearers would be influenced by His (*strength and*) ability to serve you with His life (*and not their own*).

30 And (*where you*) do not grieve the Holy Spirit of God, who has sealed you as His own (*whereby you cry Abba Father*) in the day of the redemption (*of your bodies immortal*).

31 Allowing all bitterness, and rage, and anger, screaming and yelling, and slanderous speaking, to be removed from you, (*along*) with all hatred:

32 And be kind to one another, tenderhearted (*and filled with compassion*), seeing each one as separated from the death that can animate them, even as God for Christ's sake has removed (*the sting of*) death from you.

Chapter 5

1 Therefore (*like Christ*) be followers of God (*your Father*) as His beloved children;

2 And walk (*abiding*) in (*the*) love (*of the Father*), as Christ also has (*demonstrated*) His love for us and has given Himself an

offering (*for our death*) and (*the*) sacrifice (*which God has desired from the beginning, to call upon His name*) a sweet-smelling fragrance (*to God*).

3 But fornication (*with other gods*) and all uncleanness (*which can defile the heart*) or covetousness (*which is the lust to bring forth life through my own works, which works being perishable, can never satisfy with eternal life*), let those things never be mentioned among you (*as a life*) fitting for those who are called to (*freely*) partake of God's life;

4 Neither (*let*) filthiness (*occupy your mind*), nor foolishness (*corrupt your*) speech, nor turn to (*clever*) insults, which things are (*also*) unfitting (*of the life He has set apart for you*): but rather (*set your affection upon the incorruptible life He has given you, whereby you are filled with*) thanksgiving.

5 For this we know (*and can be certain of*), that no one who runs after other gods (*worshiping the works of their own hands, which cannot ever serve them with immortality in their flesh*), nor one whose heart is defiled by iniquity (*disregarding God's gift of life in Christ for the life he can serve himself*), nor a man lusting after life by the strength contained in his flesh, who is an idolater (*in the vain worship of his own will and ability*), is able to (*ever find those things producing*) an inheritance of the kingdom of Christ and of God (*in him*).

6 (*Therefore*) let no man deceive you with idle words (*that have no benefit in their ability to produce the fruit of God's life unto immortality in your flesh*) for it is these very things which God has sworn in His wrath to destroy, which things now work in (*the hearts*) of the children who refuse to be persuaded (*to rest in God and His grace and strength to give them His blessing and life as a gift*).

7 Therefore, do not be partakers along with them (*in the way which perishes*).

8 For you were at one time (*also stumbling around*) in darkness (*blinded by death*), but now you are light (*being braided together*) with the Lord (*in union with His light and life*): walk (*then*) as (*His*) children (*born*) from the light (*of His life*):

Ephesians 5

9 For the fruit that comes from the Spirit is (*found*) inside all (*the*) goodness (*that comes from the heart of the Father*) and (*is born from*) His incorruptible life and truth (*reveal in Jesus Christ*);

10 By which we are able to discern what is (*the only life*) acceptable (*and well-pleasing*) to the Lord (*for His children*).

11 (*Therefore*) have no fellowship with the way that produces the fruit of death, but rather (*let the light that is in you*) expose it (*as the way unto death*) to those who walk in it.

12 Because it (*can bring*) shame to speak (*to them*) of those things which are done by them in secret.

13 But all things that (*can be brought to light*) are exposed and discerned by revealing the light: because whatever (*the light*) makes manifest is light.

14 This is why it is written, awake you that sleeps (*in darkness*) and arise from the dead to (*see it is*) Christ (*the light, who*) gives you (*life and*) light.

15 Giving all diligence (*to that light*) then see that you walk (*in a manner*) fitting (*of the light of His life and the hope of immortality*) and not as fools but in the wisdom (*that comes from Christ*).

16 (*Where you find His life in you*) Redeems (*back*) the time (*when you walked foolishly in death and darkness by the strength of your own hands*) because the days are filled with (*enough*) labors and annoyances (*of their own*).

17 Therefore, do not be like those who are unwise, but (*find wisdom and*) understanding (*by allowing the life that lives in Him reveal*) what the will of the Lord is (*for you*).

18 And do not be excessively drunk with *the* wine (*that the life in the world has to offer you, which has no power to serve you the life you truly desire*) but be filled with the Spirit (*which satisfies you with His life*);

19 Speaking (*comfort*) to yourselves with songs and hymns that contain the Spirit (*of life in Christ Jesus*) which brings a sweet melody to your heart from the Lord;

20 (*Where you are continuously*) filled with gratitude (*in your heart*) for all the things (*He has done*) giving thanks to our God and Father in the name of our Lord Jesus Christ;

21 Submitting yourselves one to another (*preferring each other's lives over your own*) with (*the same*) reverence of Christ.

22 Wives, be subject to your own husbands (*as one flesh*), just as (*you are one*) with the Lord.

23 Because (*as one flesh*) is the husband the head of the wife, and so also is Christ the head of (*the body*) the church (*that is one flesh*), (*Christ*) Himself being the savior of the body.

24 But like the church (*as one flesh*) is subject to Christ (*as its head*), so also are the wives to their own husbands for they are all (*part of*) the same body.

25 Husbands, love your wives (*as you do your own body*), even as Christ also loved the church, and delivered Himself up to save her;

26 So that He might sanctify (*her from death*), having cleansed the body (*from death*) through the washing of the water with the word (*declared in His resurrection from the dead*),

27 So that He might present the church (*His bride*) to Himself a glorious body, (*free from death and corruption*) not having spot or wrinkle or any such thing (*which death brought*); but that it should be set apart (*for the life He determined for them from the beginning*) and without blemish (*and free from all accusation*).

28 Even so ought husbands also love their own wives as their own bodies (*as one flesh*). For he that loves his own wife loves himself (*because they are one body*).

29 Because no man would ever hate his own body; but nourishes and cherishes it, even as Christ also nourishes and loves the church;

30 For we are all members of His body.

31 And for this reason will a man leave his father and mother and join himself to his wife; and the two will become one flesh.

32 This is a great mystery: which I am speaking regarding Christ and the church (*how He has joined Himself as one flesh to us, absorbing our death and giving us His life*).

Ephesians 6

33 Nevertheless, let each one of you (*husbands*) love his own wife as he does his own body; and (*also*) the wife see that she (*as one flesh*), respect her husband (*as one in the Lord*).

Chapter 6

1 Children, listen carefully to observe (*the instructions of*) your parents regarding the Lord: for this is how (*God designed*) that it should be.

2 That you (*like Christ, would*) honor (*and cherish above all things, the instruction of Abba*) your Father and (*the Holy Spirit, who is wonderful counselor, your*) mother; which is the first precept that points to the promise (*of eternal life*);

3 That (*He would be with you to father you with His life*) which (*life is*) well pleasing to you, and so that you may live long in the land (*which the Lord has promised to give you as an inheritance and serve you with kindness for all the ages to come, in a world without end*).

4 And you, (*earthly*) fathers, do not (*deal impatiently*), angering your children to wrath (*which has no ability to produce the fruit of God's life in them*), but bring them up in the training and correction which comes from (*the faith authored and finished*) by the Lord (*Jesus*).

5 To them which are under the authority of others, listen carefully to follow the instructions of those whom you serve according to the flesh, with fear and trembling (*which is to stand in awe of and totally rely upon the Father's ability and not your own*), with singleness (*and sincerity*) of your heart (*and mind*), according to (*the wisdom of*) Christ;

6 Not just with service that can be seen with the eyes which only pleases men but as those who are being served by the life of Christ (*giving all diligence to the faith of Christ*), which is to do the will of God from the heart;

7 With kindness do your service (*from the heart*) as the Lord (*has persuaded you*) and not (*with eyeservice*) to (*please*) men:

8 Knowing that whatever good thing any man does, the same (*finds its origin in that which*) he has received from the Lord, whether he is bound or free.

9 And you who have rule over others, do the same things (*with kindness*) toward those who are under your authority (*having your heart persuaded by the Lord*), (*where you are able to*) let go of threatening: knowing that your Master in heaven (*has served you with kindness*); neither does He make any distinction between those who are bound or free (*Jew or Gentile, male or female*).

10 Finally, my brethren, be strengthened (*abiding*) in the Lord (*by looking unto Him as your strength*) and in the power of His might (*and not your own*).

11 Being (*fully*) clothed with the armor of God (*which He desires*) to clothe you with, so that you may be able to stand (*in the power of His might and not your own*) against the craftily devised schemes (*which have been planted in the world by that slanderous accuser*) the devil.

12 For we do not wrestle against (*nor is our conflict with*) flesh and blood (*fighting against other men in the flesh*), but against the rulers and against powers (*of darkness*), against the vital principles of iniquity (*and its pain ridden ordinances to serve yourself with a good life*) which are exalted (*and contained*) in the world.

13 Because of this (*grab hold of*) taking unto yourself the complete armor (*which you have received*) from God, so that you may (*by the power of His might*) withstand the day when you are pressed in and harassed (*and abused*) by the labors (*and annoyances that death can bring*) and having done all (*this*) to (*rest*) established (*in Him who has already stood in the face of death for you*).

14 Stand therefore (*resting and established*) in the truth which contains the power to reproduce His life (*and immortality*) in you, and clothed with the breastplate (*that protects your heart with His loving-kindness, persuading you*) of His indestructible life (*where you are free from death and the fear of death*);

Ephesians 6

15 And your feet firmly established in (*the certainty of the word*) the gospel declares (*which was made flesh in the resurrection, the hope of the same life of Christ that came out of the grave an immortal man which word serves our hearts with love*) peace (*and rest that brings unity*);

16 Above everything else, diligently harken to the faith (*of our Lord Jesus*) which (*is full of power and ability to*) shield you from and extinguish all the fiery darts that death can bring (*by beholding that death has been abolished in the testimony of Jesus Christ*).

17 And receive (*Christ who is*) the helmet (*the head that provides all nourishment to the body and the hope*) of (*our*) salvation (*and wholeness, who has sent away death and brought His life and immortality to light*) and the sword of the Spirit, which speaks the word of God (*to your heart whereby you cry, Abba Father*):

18 Praying on every occasion and with each type of prayer and request by the Spirit (*interceding in our hearts*), looking (*only*) to (*Him*) with steadfastness (*the One who has provided Himself*) for the needs of all the saints;

19 And (*pray*) for me, that (*the Spirit*) would provide me the words, so that I may open my mouth boldly, to (*declare and*) make known the mystery of the gospel (*in Christ*),

20 For which I am an ambassador in (*light*) chains (*which contain no ability to injure my life in Christ*): so that in these bonds I may speak (*with*) boldness (*and confidence*) the things which I ought to speak.

21 But (*also*) so that you may know my affairs, and how I am doing, Tych'i-cus, a beloved brother (*of mine*) and faithful minister in the Lord, will make all these things known to you:

22 I have sent him to you for the same purpose, so that you might know our affairs, and that (*in doing so*) he might comfort your hearts.

23 Peace be with all the brethren, and love along with the faith, (*which comes*) from God the Father and the Lord Jesus Christ.

24 (*May the*) grace (*which comes from God influence the hearts of*) all of them who love our Lord Jesus Christ with (*His*) immortality. Amen.

The Epistle of Paul to the

PHILIPPIANS

The Faith Translation

Chapter 1

1 Paul and Timothy, the servants of (*the faith of*) Jesus Christ, to all those who are sharers fellowshipping (*in the same life revealed*) in Christ Jesus (*our Lord*) which are at Philippi, along with the overseers and deacons (*appointed to your assembly*).

2 (*May His*) Grace (*be multiplied*) to you and peace from God our Father and from the Lord Jesus Christ.

3 I (*give*) thanks to my God every time I think of you,

4 Always making all my prayers for you with great joy,

5 Because of your fellowship (*with me*) in the gospel from the first day (*you heard it*) until now;

6 Being fully persuaded of this very thing, that the One who has brought forth His life (*and inner desire*) in you will (*also*) bring it to completion (*in the glorification of your bodies*) in the day of Jesus Christ' (*return*):

7 And it seems right for me to think these things about you all, because I have you in my heart; both in my imprisonment and in the defense and establishing of the gospel, since you are all partakers along with me of the grace of God (*according to the gospel which I delivered to you*).

8 For God is my witness, how (*His love has compelled me*), earnestly desiring for you all (*to experience His life*) with the (*same*) tender compassion of Jesus Christ.

9 And this I pray (*also for you*), so that your love may abound (*one for another*), more and more in the knowledge (*of Christ Jesus*) and in (*His*) judgment of all things;

10 So that you may (*thereby examine all things*) and discern the things which are (*good and*) excellent (*according to His judgment unto life*); so that you may be pure and blameless unto the coming of Jesus Christ;

11 And being filled with the fruits of His incorruptible life, which are from abiding in (*the faith of*) Jesus Christ and is that which brings glory and speaks well of God (*our Father*).

Philippians 1

12 But I want you to know brethren, that the things which have come against me really turned out to the advancement of the gospel;

13 So that (*because of*) my imprisonment for (*preaching*) Christ (*has the gospel*) become clearly known (*even*) in the palaces (*of kings and world leaders*) and in all other places;

14 And many brethren (*who trust*) in the Lord, have gained in confidence because of my imprisonment, daring to speak more abundantly and fearlessly the word of God (*in Christ*).

15 And yet (*I know that*) some preach out of jealousy (*of my ministry*) and their desire to debate (*and be argumentative*); while others (*simply*) proclaim Christ from the overflow of His goodness and mercy in their hearts:

16 The one preaches Christ out of selfish ambition and not from pure motives (*but mixed with their own desires*), thinking that it will make my chains more distressful:

17 But the others (*preach*) out of the love (*of God in their hearts for all people, that compels them to do so*), knowing that I (*have settled in my heart and*) am destined (*and willing to lay down my life*) in defense of the gospel (*which we preach*).

18 What do I think about these things? Only that in every way, whether from impure motives or a heart persuaded of the truth is Christ being proclaimed; and that (*makes my heart*) rejoice, and yes, I certainly will rejoice.

19 Because I know that (*my bonds*) will turn out to (*further declare the truth of the gospel*) of my salvation through your prayers and the abundant supply of the Spirit of Jesus Christ,

20 And according to my confident expectation and certainty (*of the life revealed in Christ Jesus*), (*which is*) my hope, so that in nothing will I be ashamed, but will continue with all boldness (*to declare the gospel*) where in Christ will be magnified in my body, whether it be by (*His*) life or (*my*) death.

21 Because for me to live (*in the flesh*) is (*to live having*) Christ' (*life in me*) and to die (*and be with Christ is*) gain.

22 But if I (*continue to*) live in the flesh, (*it is His life that lives in me and*) the fruit (*of His life*) which occupies and works in me: yet which I would choose I do not know.

23 Because I am hard-pressed to choose between the two, having a desire to depart and be with Christ which is much better (*for me*):

24 But despite that for me to remain in the flesh seems more of a necessity for you.

25 And seeing as I know (*it would be more helpful for you*), I will remain and continue with you (*constantly reminding*) you all (*of the gospel of Christ*), for your profit and the joy (*which comes from the hearing*) of faith;

26 So that your boasting might be in Jesus Christ (*and not in me*) when I come to you again.

27 Where you allow your life to be (*born from the faith of Him*) suitable of the same quality and value brought (*to you*) by the gospel of Christ: so that whether I come to see you, or am absent from you, I might hear the things concerning you, that you stand (*finding your life born from the same*) spirit and mind (*of Christ*), diligently seeking together the faith of the gospel;

28 And (*where*) you are not frightened by those (*in the world*) who oppose you (*in the faith*): which to them is the evidence of sure destruction (*to stand still and not lift a finger to preserve their own lives*) but to you (*it is*) salvation (*from death and destruction*) and unto an indestructible life which is (*freely given to you*) of God.

29 For unto you it has been given (*so that you may rest in*) Christ, not only believing upon (*the life of*) Him (*that came out of the grave*) but also to suffer in the world (*knowing that you also possess a life that cannot be hurt or injured by the death in the world*) because of Him;

30 And (*you also share in*) this same conflict (*of faith*) you see in me and have now heard of me.

Chapter 2

1 If then the (*same*) faith that was in Christ has come to exhort (*and persuade our hearts*), if all comfort (*is found*) in (*being persuaded of His*) love, if (*it is also what brings*) fellowship with

Philippians 2

the Spirit, and if (*Christ is where*) all (*the same*) compassions and mercies (*come forth in us*),

2 Then the fulfillment of my joy (*for you*) is that you all be of the same mind (*as Christ*), having the same love (*born in you*), and being united in one mind (*and one spirit*).

3 (*Where*) nothing (*you do*) is from selfish ambition (*and strife*) or a high opinion of oneself; but (*rather where*) thinking little of your ability (*and much of God's*) to exalt you to blessing and life, you esteem others above yourselves.

4 Where every man is not considering his own welfare but preferring (*and caring for the welfare of*) others.

5 Allow (*yourself, therefore, to be persuaded by the faith of Christ Jesus*) so that this (*same*) mind would be in you, which was also in Him:

6 Who, already possessing the life of God in Himself did not think it was something He needed to seize upon (*and attain to by force*) already being equal with God:

7 But (*preferring our life over His own*) made Himself of no reputation (*laying aside His life*) taking the form of a servant and was made in the likeness of (*corruptible*) men.

8 And finding Himself (*the Son spoken of in the volume of the book*) in the same body (*and shape*) as corruptible man, He dismissed any reliance upon Himself (*to be exalted but trusted solely upon the Father*) and (*being filled with the desire to do His will*) He, (*for the joy that was set before Him*) became obedient (*in offering His body*) unto death, even the death of the cross.

9 Therefore has God Himself also highly exalted Him (*to His right hand, in immortal flesh and bone, far surpassing all wisdom, knowledge and authority*), and (*has shown forth His lovingkindness He has toward man*) in giving Him (*the Son of man*) a name which is above every name:

10 So that at the name of Jesus every knee (*that would exalt itself above the wisdom of God*) would have to bow down, of those things which are in heaven and those in earth as well as the (*death and corruption*) which was planted in the earth.

11 And every tongue (*that has ever come to accuse man that he was not the son*) would have to bow in submission, agreeing that Jesus Christ is Lord (*over all flesh, having conquered death in the flesh*), unto the glorification of His body immortal (*declaring the good opinion and value of man that*) God the Father (*has had from the beginning*).

12 Therefore my beloved, just as you have always hearkened diligently to be obedient to the faith (*of Jesus Christ*) not only when I was with you but now much more in my absence (*may each one of you allow this faith to*) work out salvation in your own hearts with fear and trembling (*which is to fully rely on Him and His ability to serve you with an indestructible life and not your own*).

13 For it is God (*and the word that He has spoken in Christ*) that works in your heart both to (*bring about His*) desire and (*He alone is fully able*) and takes great pleasure to perform it (*in you*).

14 Do all things (*cheerfully*) without murmuring (*in secret displeasure*) and inward debate.

15 So that you may appear blameless and innocent, the sons of God, unblemished (*from the marring effects brought by death*), in the midst of a twisted and perverse generation among whom you shine as lights in the world (*which is still filled with death and darkness*);

16 Having been marked by the word of life; so that I may rejoice (*glorying*) in the day of Christ, (*knowing*) that I did not run my race without profit, neither have I labored (*for the truth*) in vain.

17 And (*in fact*) even if I am offered (*and my blood is poured out*) in a sacrifice and for the ministration of the faith to you, I (*will have*) joy and will rejoice with you all.

18 And likewise it is the same (*faith*) which also causes you to have joy and rejoice with me.

19 But I trust in the Lord Jesus (*and hope*) to send Timothy to you shortly, so that I also will be encouraged when I hear the things concerning you.

Philippians 3

20 Because I do not know of anyone (*else*) who is as likeminded (*as myself*) who will genuinely care for you.

21 For all seek their own (*personal interest*) and not the things which are in Jesus Christ.

22 But you know (*and have seen*) the evidence of him, (*how*) that like a son with the father, he has served with me in the gospel.

23 For that reason it is him that I hope to send you immediately, as soon as I see how things will go for me.

24 But I am persuaded in the Lord (*hoping*) that I as well might come to you shortly.

25 Yet (*it seemed good and*) I considered it necessary to send to you E-paph-ro-di'tus, my brother (*in Christ*), and companion in (*the work of the*) ministry, and fellow associate, but also your messenger and he that ministered to my needs.

26 For he has great affection for you all, and was deeply distressed (*by your sorrow*), because you had heard that he had been sick.

27 For indeed he was sick and near to death: but God had mercy on him; and not on him only, but on me also, lest I should have sorrow on sorrow.

28 Therefore I have sent him more speedily, so you would be able to see him again and so that you may rejoice, and I may be less sorrowful.

29 Receive him therefore in the Lord with all gladness; and hold him in high regard:

30 Because (*it was*) for the work of Christ (*that*) he was near to death, not regarding his (*own*) life, (*but he came to me in your place*) to supply for my needs because of your lack of opportunity toward me (*seeing I could not be with you in person*).

Chapter 3

1 Finally my brethren (*in Christ*), rejoice in (*and find your delight*) in the Lord (*who is the source of all joy*). For me, it is not troublesome to write to you (*again and remind you of*) the

56

same things, on the other hand for you (*to hear and keep on hearing*) is a safeguard (*from being led astray*).

2 Beware of dogs (*who are of a corrupt mindset outside of the faith of Jesus Christ*), beware of those whose works are born from the serpent, beware of the false circumcision (*made with man's hands who glory in their flesh*).

3 For we are the true circumcision, who trust in (*and rely upon*) the Spirit of God (*to serve us with the life that is*) in Christ Jesus (*our Lord*) in whom we rejoice and have no confidence in the flesh (*to preserve our lives from the death in the world*).

4 Although I could find reasons to have confidence in the flesh. If any other man thinks that he has reasons that he might trust in his flesh, I have even more:

5 I was circumcised (*in my flesh*) on the eighth day, from the offspring of Israel, of the tribe of Benjamin, a Hebrew of Hebrews; according to the law (*I was of the separatist sect*) a Pharisee.

6 I displayed my enthusiasm (*and fervor*), by pursuing to apprehend and overtake the church; according to the deeds of the law (*did I keep myself ceremonially clean and*) blameless.

7 But whatever things I formerly thought were gain to me (*in the flesh and in the world*), those things I (*now*) consider a total loss for (*the purpose of obtaining to the incorruptible life revealed in*) Christ Jesus our Lord.

8 Yes and in fact, I consider all things (*that I could have ever gained by my flesh*) nothing but loss for (*the purpose of obtaining to and compared to*) the (*surpassing*) excellency of the knowledge of Christ Jesus my Lord: because of (*the revelation of*) Him (*and His life and immortality*) I have suffered the loss of all those things (*which I previously labored to gain by my flesh*) and I count them completely worthless (*and only fit to be discarded as filthy waste*), so that I may gain (*the inheritance of eternal life in*) Christ (*Jesus my Lord*),

9 And be found (*resting*) in Him, not having the (*corruptible*) life (*that I can gather to myself by the flesh*), which is by (*laboring to keep*) the carnal commandments contained in the

57

law, but that incorruptible life which is through (*resting in*) the faith (*that was authored and finished in the death, burial, and resurrection*) of Christ, (*being persuaded by*) the life (*which God has promised from the beginning and has come out of the grave immortal by the faith*) revealed by God in Christ:

10 So that I may be intimately acquainted (*and intertwined with*) Him, and (*the hope of*) the (*glorious*) power of His resurrection, and (*that by sharing*) in the fellowship of His suffering (*where He did not lift one finger to preserve His own life but trusted in the Father*), (*that my heart would also rest in Him*) being formed into the same image (*as His and the*) death (*that He died*);

11 So that in that same manner (*as Him*) I might attain to the resurrection of the dead.

12 Not that I have already attained to the thing which my heart (*finds certainty in and*) hopes for or have already been made perfect (*in my body immortal*), but I follow after (*the faith of Christ*), so that I may lay hold of the (*life and immortality*) which (*God has purposed and promised from the beginning*) for which my heart has also been grabbed hold of by in Christ Jesus.

13 Brethren, I do not consider myself to have (*already*) obtained to (*the resurrection and redemption of my body*): but this one thing I do, forgetting (*the death that once reigned over me and*) those things which are (*now*) behind (*me*), I reach forward to the sure hope (*of the same life that is in Christ Jesus my Lord*) that is before (*me*),

14 I pursue (*the life which my heart has always desired, which is also*) the mark (*that God has fixed His eyes on for my life from the beginning*) and toward the prize He has called me to, with the (*most eloquent speech and the*) highest calling of God in Christ Jesus.

15 Therefore, as many as (*desire*) to be perfect (*as He is perfect*), be of the same mind (*seeing that you lack nothing*): and if in anything you are of a different mind, (*it is*) God (*who*) will also reveal (*and bring to light*) even this to you.

16 But regarding that which we have already attained to (*and seen in Christ*), let us walk (*being persuaded*) by the same mind (*revealed in the faith of Jesus Christ*), let us be diligent to be mindful of the same.

17 Brethren be followers (*of His faith*) together with me and consider those who (*also*) walk like me (*seeing*) as you have us for an example.

18 Because many (*in the world*) walk; of whom I have often told you and even now do with (*great sorrow and*) tears in my eyes, that they walk as enemies (*standing opposed to*) the cross of Christ (*and instead glorying in the life they can gather to themselves in the world*):

19 Where their end is destruction, and their god is their belly (*feeding their flesh with that which can never satisfy its lust for life*), and who esteem that which only serves them with shame, who mind earthly things.

20 (*But follow our example*) because the life that we possess in us (*even now in this world*) is seated at the right hand of the Father in heaven (*inside immortal human flesh*); from where we look for (*the certainty, of the same life in our body in the return of*) the Savior, the Lord Jesus Christ:

21 Who will transform our vile (*corruptible*) body, so that it may be formed into the image and likeness of His glorified (*incorruptible*) body, through His doing and power (*alone*) by which (*power and dominion*) He is able even to subdue all things (*in heaven and in earth*) unto Himself.

Chapter 4

1 Therefore, my brethren, my dearly beloved and greatly missed, my joy and crown, stand firm in the Lord (*and the certainty of all He has done*), my beloved.

2 I exhort Eu-o'di-as, and exhort Syn'ty-che, that they would be of the same mind in the Lord.

3 And I earnestly request that you also, my true partners, help these women who have labored together with me in the gospel,

Philippians 4

along with Clem'ent and with my other fellow workers, whose names are written in the book of life.

4 Rejoice (*and delight yourself*) in (*all that*) the Lord (*has done*) always (*being mindful of it*): and again, I say, rejoice.

5 Let your gentleness (*and patience*) be known to all men. The Lord is (*always*) near (*unto you*).

6 (*Therefore*) do not be anxious (*thinking that you must take great care for your own life and future*) but in every situation (*when the word that death can bring comes with its laborious and abusive thoughts to your heart and mind*) it is by prayer (*an exchange of your inner desires with His*) by earnestly crying out to the One who supplies (*all your needs in Christ, by whom also you see He has already conquered your death, so that with your heart being filled*) with thanksgiving, you let your desire made known to God.

7 And the peace (*that comes from seeing your death has been conquered can only come*) from God, which (*peace*) surpasses all understanding (*that is in the world*) and will keep your hearts and minds (*free from these laborious imaginations and tormenting thoughts*) through Christ Jesus.

8 Finally my brethren, whatever is true, whatever is honorable, whatever is just, whatever is pure, whatever is admirable, if anything be good and virtuous, and if anything, be praiseworthy, think on these things.

9 And (*as you think on*) these things which you have learned, and received, and heard and seen in me, walk also in the same: and the God who serves you with (*life and*) peace will always be with you.

10 But I am so grateful to the Lord, that now, after some time you have sent care for me again; it is not that you were not always concerned for me, but you lacked opportunity.

11 And I am not saying that I was destitute (*and lacking in what I needed for contentment*): because (*as I have grown in the knowledge of Him*) I have learned that whatever circumstances I find myself in (*that He is the sufficiency for my life and being persuaded of that*) I am fully content.

12 I (*have both experienced and*) know what it is like to be brought low and what it is like to flourish: In every (*circumstance*) and in all things, I have learned the secret (*of contentment is in Him*), whether I am full or hungry, both when in abundance or in need.

13 For in all these things I find (*that the*) strength (*for me to experience all the fruit of His life with contentment is only found*) in Christ, the One who strengthens me.

14 But you have done a beautiful thing, having fellowship in my affliction.

15 Now you Phi-lip'pi-ans should also know that in the beginning of the gospel when I went out from Mac-e-do'ni-a, there was no other church that shared with me, giving and receiving for my needs but you alone.

16 And even (*when I was*) in Thes-sa-lo-ni'ca you sent once and then again (*contributing*) to my needs.

17 I am not seeking after the gift: but my desire (*is for you to experience*) the (*incorruptible*) fruit (*God supplies*) that is (*already*) overflowing to your account (*and in your lives*).

18 Now I have all that I need, and more: I have received in full (*the supplies*) from E-paph-ro-di'tus which you sent to me; (*which offering was like*) a sweet-smelling fragrance, a sacrifice (*which comes from hearts overflowing with the fruit of His life*) which is acceptable and well pleasing to God.

19 And my God (*is the One*) who will supply all of your needs (*for life and Godlikeness*) according to the abundant supply of His incorruptible life through Christ Jesus (*our Lord*).

20 Now all the glory be unto God and our Father forever and ever. Amen.

21 Greet all those fellowshipping with us in the life of Christ Jesus. The brethren which are with me greet you.

22 All the believers here greet you, especially those that are of the household of Caesar.

23 The grace (*that comes*) from our Lord Jesus Christ be with all your lives. Amen.

The Epistle of Paul to the

COLOSSIANS

The Faith Translation

Chapter 1

1 Paul, an apostle (*and messenger of the gospel*) of Jesus Christ by the will of God, and Timothy our brother,

2 To those who have been set apart (*for His life*), the believing brethren (*who share in the faith*) of Christ which are at Colos'se: (*His*) grace be with you and the peace which comes from God our Father and the Lord Jesus Christ.

3 We give thanks to the God and Father of our Lord Jesus Christ, praying for you continually,

4 Having heard of the faith you share in Christ Jesus, and the love that you have towards all the fellow believers there,

5 Because of the (*sure*) hope that is reserved for you in (*Christ Jesus*) in the heavens, which you have heard in the word of truth of the gospel;

6 Which (*truth*) has come to you, as it has in all the world bearing fruit and increasing, as it also has in you since the day you heard and knew (*with certainty*) the blessing and life that has been brought to you (*by Jesus Christ*) from God in truth;

7 Just as you have learned from Ep'a-phras our beloved fellow worker (*in the gospel*), who is a trustworthy minister of Christ on our behalf,

8 Who has also declared to us your love (*which fruit*) the Spirit (*has brought forth in you*).

9 For this reason also since the day we heard of your love, we have not ceased praying for you, asking that you would be filled full (*knowing that you are complete in Him*) in the knowledge of His will (*to give you His blessing and life as an inheritance*) and in all spiritual wisdom and understanding (*which comes from being persuaded of that*),

10 So that you might walk in a manner that is fitting of the life which the Lord takes pleasure to serve you with, and in every good work (*which He has prepared beforehand for you to walk in*) bearing the fruit (*of His life*) and in the knowledge of God;

Colossians 1

11 Strengthened with all power (*in the inner man with hope*), according to the might (*and strength displayed*) in His glory, which (*brings forth*) all patience and longsuffering with joy;

12 Giving thanks to the Father, who formed us (*in His image*) so that we might be partakers of the inheritance that He has set apart for His children (*to stand before Him*) in the light (*of His life*):

13 Who has delivered us from the power of death and darkness, and has translated us (*from death and corruption*) unto the kingdom (*of light and life*) of the Son in His love;

14 In whom we have redemption (*from death*) through His blood, divorcing us from the death (*which held us in bondage all our days, through the fear of death, to labor and toil in our flesh to preserve our own lives*):

15 Who is the (*expressed and exact image*) of the invisible God (*in immortal flesh and bone*), the firstborn (*from the dead*) of every creature:

16 Because by Him were all things created, that are in heaven, and that are in earth, visible and invisible, whether they be thrones (*where kings are seated with footstools*), or dominion (*powers that exert authority*), or the origin of all rulership, or powers: (*the beginning of*) all things that were created (*were created*) by Him, and for Him:

17 And He is (*the Alpha and the Omega, the One who is, who was*) before all things (*and who is to come*), and by Him do all things exist (*and are held together*).

18 And He is (*and will forever be*) the head of the body, the church: who is the beginning (*and the completion of creation*), the firstborn from the dead; so that in all things He might hold preeminence (*the chief place of influence*).

19 For it pleased the Father that in Him should all the fullness (*of the Godhead*) dwell (*bodily*);

20 And, having made peace (*and unity between those were far off and those who were near to God*) through the blood of His cross (*by destroying the death that was against them both in His flesh*), by Him (*in order*) to reconcile (*and unite*) all things

64

(*back*) to Himself; by Him, I say, whether they be things in earth, or things in heaven.

21 And you (*Gentiles*), who were at one time excluded (*from the commonwealth of Israel feeling estranged from the promises, having no hope*) and openly hostile (*toward God*) the understanding of your minds darkened through your wicked imaginations (*to preserve your own lives*), yet now has He reconciled (*you and united all men in the one new man Christ Jesus*)

22 In the body of His flesh through (*the*) death (*of death*), to present you (*His children*) set apart (*for His life*) and unblemished (*from death's marring effects*) and blameless (*from any accusation*) before Him (*in His love*):

23 If you abide in the faith (*revealed in Jesus Christ*) established and settled (*in it*), and (*so that you are*) not able to be moved from the hope of the gospel (*which is the certainty of the same life*), which you have heard, and which was declared (*in the death, burial, resurrection and ascension of Jesus Christ*) to every creature which is under heaven; whereof I, Paul am made a minister;

24 And even now do I rejoice for you in (*the midst of*) my afflictions, and being filled up (*complete in Him, and coming behind in no good thing*) sharing in the sufferings of Christ in my flesh (*which He suffered*) for His body's sake, which is the church:

25 Of which I am made a minister, according to the administration of God which He has given me for you (*in the revelation of Jesus Christ*), to fulfill the word of God;

26 Even the mystery which has been hidden (*in Christ*) from ages and generations but now has been made manifest to (*us*) His saints (*in the word made immortal flesh in Jesus Christ*):

27 To (*us*) who God would reveal (*in His Son made immortal flesh*) what is the riches of the glory of this mystery (*even*) among the Gentiles, which is (*the life of*) Christ (*abiding*) in you, the hope of glory (*which is the certainty of the same life and immortality revealed in His resurrection in immortal flesh and bone*):

Colossians 2

28 (*Christ*) who we preach (*and who is the very logic of God*) by which we reason with every man, teaching every man in all wisdom (*through Him who is the full counsel and wisdom of God*): so that we may prove to every man (*that their*) perfection (*is only found*) in Christ Jesus:

29 And (*who is the wisdom from which*) I also labor (*in the gospel*), according to the wisdom and knowledge of Him which works mightily in me.

Chapter 2

1 For I would like you to know how great a fight (*of passion*) I have for you and for those who are in La-od-i-ce'a and even for all those who have never seen my face in person.

2 That their hearts may be comforted (*and encouraged*), having been braided together in (*His*) love, and into all the riches (*of His glory*) from the certainty (*and confidence*) that comes from understanding unto the knowledge of the mystery of God that is (*revealed*) in Christ;

3 In whom all the treasures of wisdom and knowledge (*which can be found*) are hidden.

4 And I say this so that no man may deceive you with persuasive (*but misleading*) words.

5 Because even though I am absent in the flesh, I am with you in the spirit, and I rejoice in seeing the way you order your lives and how that you have the solid foundation of your faith in Christ.

6 In the same way therefore that you have received Christ Jesus the Lord (*by hearing the faith*), walk, the same way (*by continually hearing the faith*) of Him:

7 Being planted firmly and built up (*in the faith of*) Him and being established (*and strengthened*) in the faith just as you were taught (*of Him*), (*with that which makes your cup*) overflow with thanksgiving.

8 Take heed (*to hear and keep on hearing the faith*) so that no man is able to take you captive through philosophy (*and the love of their own wisdom*) and (*with*) empty (*worthless*)

deceitful words, (*which are*) according to the traditions of men, and founded upon the basic principles contained in the world (*being subject to its ordinances of touch not, taste not, handle not*) and not according to (*the faith contained in*) Jesus Christ.

9 Because in Him dwells all the fullness of the Godhead in (*an immortal flesh and bone*) body.

10 And you are complete in Him (*lacking nothing you need for His life and Godlikeness*), who is the head of all rule and authority:

11 In whom also you are circumcised with the circumcision made without hands, in cutting off the body of death in the flesh by the circumcision of Christ (*in condemning death in the flesh*):

12 Buried with Him in (*the*) baptism (*of His death*), wherein you also are risen with Him (*to new life*) through the faith of the righteous act of God, the One who has raised Him from the dead.

13 And while you were yet dead in the offenses (*that came through the death that entered into the world and reigned over you, causing you to deviate from the truth, laboring in vain to preserve your own life*) in your uncircumcised (*dying*) flesh, He has quickened you together (*to new life*) with Him, having sent away from you (*the death that reigned over you and which was the cause of*) all offenses;

14 Blotting out (*the debt of offenses that were created, contained in*) the handwritten ordinances (*which death used to accuse our hearts by the law of commandments and in the basic principles of the world*) that were against us, which were contrary (*to the way unto life and*) to us (*having the incorruptible life He designed us for*), and He took them out of the way in destroying death (*abolishing it in His flesh*), nailing it to the cross (*like the proclamation of a debt that's been settled*);

15 And having (*done so He*) disarmed all rulers and authorities (*stripping them of the weapon they used to deceive*), putting it on open display, showing (*that the end of*) their way only leads

to death, (*and how that He*) triumphed over death (*in the victory*) of the cross (*being raised immortal*).

16 Therefore let no man judge you by (*the*) meat (*you eat or avoid*), or by (*the*) drink (*you drink or avoid*), or in regard to (*setting apart certain*) days as holy, such as the (*day of a*) new moon, or about the sabbath days (*but only by Christ*):

17 (*Because*) all these things (*were given as*) a foreshadow (*pointing to*) things to come; but the substance (*of them*) is Christ.

18 Let no man deprive (*or disqualify*) you from your reward (*which is freely given in Christ*), (*from one*) coming (*to you*) with a false humility and giving (*more*) reverence to angels (*than is due*), and going into details regarding things which he has never seen, having an inflated (*view of himself*) without cause through (*the knowledge of good and evil*) in his carnal mind,

19 And not beholding (*and grabbing hold of*) the Head (*who is Christ*), from where all the (*members of the*) body (*which is the church*) with its joints and ligaments are supplied (*and receive*) the food (*and nourishment*) that ministers (*His life*), and knits (*them*) together (*in His love*) and increases with increased (*fruit*) which comes from God.

20 Therefore if you are dead with Christ from the basic principles of the world, why (*would you live*) as though your life is still found in the world, being subject to its ordinances of,

21 (Touch not; taste not; handle not;

22 Which all are to (*decay and*) perish with use;) according to the (*carnal*) commandments and doctrines of men?

23 Which things do have the appearance of wisdom in the worship of your own will power (*which is self-worship that cannot ever bring forth the life and the fruit of God*), in false humility, and in harsh treatment of the body: not having any value (*in its ability*) to (*ever truly*) satisfy the flesh (*to go to rest in the certainty of immortality*).

Chapter 3

1 If then you have been raised with Christ, seek (*meditate and reason on*) those things which are above, (*in heaven*) where Christ sits (*in a glorified human body*) on the right hand of God.

2 Set your mind (*and affection*) on (*the incorruptible*) things (*in heaven*) above, not on (*the corruptible*) things on the earth.

3 Because you are dead (*to the corruptible life in the world*), and your life is hidden (*incorruptible*) with Christ in God (*undefiled and where it cannot ever fade away*).

4 Therefore when Christ is revealed (*from heaven*) with the life (*and inheritance*) which He has reserved for you, then will you also appear (*in history*) with Him (*the sons of God*) in (*the same life and*) glory (*in immortality*).

5 Consider therefore the (*corruptible*) members (*contained in your flesh*) which are upon the earth, already dead (*in the death you died with Christ, along with the fruit of death which they can sting you with*); fornication (*being intimate with the works of your hands*), uncleanness (*touching death*), consumed by excessive (*and tormenting*) passions, an unrestrained lust (*for the life you can gather to yourself*), and covetousness, (*always greedily desiring for more and never quenching that feeling you lack*), which things are idolatry (*that set up the works of your hands as your god unto your own destruction*):

6 For this reason has God sworn in His wrath to destroy death (*taking vengeance upon*) those things which come upon the children who refuse to be persuaded (*that He conquered their death and has given them His life so that they might cease from those things which only lead to destruction*):

7 In those things which you also walked at one time (*in the way that leads to destruction*), when you lived (*as the old man, being dead and laboring for life in vain according to the strength contained*) in your dying flesh.

8 But now (*as the new man who is dead to death*) lay aside (*and no longer consider the weakness in your flesh which*

Colossians 3

formerly worked in your members to produce) anger, *(outbursts of)* rage, hatred, slanderous lies *(against God)*, speaking *(with filthy communication)* the lies that dwell in your heart out of your mouth.

9 *(But now knowing the truth)* do not *(speak)* lies to one another seeing as you have laid aside *(and considered)* the old man *(dead)* along with his deeds *(which were animated by the death that reigned over him)*;

10 And now you have considered yourself *(made alive in Him and)* clothed upon by the new man *(who can never die)*, which *(through the knowledge of Christ)* has renewed *(man back)* to the image of Him that created him *(to be a partaker of His life and immortality)*:

11 Where there is no *(distinction between)* Greek or Jew, circumcision, or uncircumcision, *(uncivilized)* Bar-ba'ri-an, savage, slave or free: but *(only)* Christ *(who)* is *(for)* all, and in all.

12 Be clothed upon therefore *(with His life)* knowing that God has always purposed and desired it for you *(from the beginning)* setting you apart *(for that life)* and *(even when you were dead)* loving you in the bowels of His tender mercies *(to serve you with all the fruit of His life)* kindness, humbleness of mind, meekness, longsuffering;

13 *(Whereby you can come alongside)* having patience with one another's *(faults)* and forgiving one another, *(so that)* if any man has a conflict with another: just as Christ has sent away *(and divorced you from death)*, *(seeing them in Christ separated from death)* you also would send away *(not crediting)* their offense *(to their account)*.

14 And above all things be clothed upon with His life *(allowing Him to serve you)* with His love, *(which love)* is the very thing that braids us together with Him in perfection.

15 And allow the peace *(and rest)* that comes from God *(and from abiding in His life)* to rule in our hearts *(presiding over our lives)*, unto the life and peace which He has also called you and united us in one body and *(where you may be ever)* filled with gratefulness *(and thanksgiving)*.

16 Allow (*therefore*) the word (*that God has spoken in*) Christ to abide in you abundantly (*where you are fully supplied with*) all wisdom; teaching and encouraging (*yourself and*) one another with psalms and hymns and songs that impart the spirit of faith, singing to the Lord (*with gratitude*) about the blessing and life (*He has influenced upon*) your hearts (*through Jesus Christ*).

17 And (*so that*) in whatever things (*you may be occupied*) whether it is in word or in doings, that they all may (*be persuaded by Him*) giving all glory to (*and exalting*) the name of the Lord Jesus, giving thanks to God and to the Father (*who brings forth His life in us*) through Him.

18 Wives, submit yourselves (*as one flesh in union*) to your own husbands, just as you are (*one body*) in (*union with*) the Lord.

19 Husbands, love your wives (*just as Christ loves us, seeing we are bone of His bone and flesh of His flesh*), and (*where in seeing you are one flesh*) you are not harsh (*impatient or bitter*) toward them.

20 Children, obey (*listening diligently*) to your parents in all things: for this (*same diligence*) is well pleasing to (*those who as little children hearken to*) the Lord (*and His instruction unto life*).

21 Fathers, do not provoke your children (*to anger*), (*but let your correction nurture them with the life and the hope that is in Christ*) so that you do not discourage them.

22 Servants, (*listen carefully to*) follow (*the instructions of*) your masters in all things according to the flesh; not just with (*the obedience*) that can be seen with the eye, which only pleases men; but with the singleness (*and sincerity*) of the heart which (*gives all diligence to the faith of our Lord Jesus*) totally reliant upon Him in reverence to God;

23 And (*where*) whatever you do, (*you would*) do (*from a*) heart (*that being born of the Spirit has been stung by His life*), as (*one giving glory*) to the Lord, and not to that which (*only exalts and*) pleases men;

Colossians 4

24 Knowing (*with certainty*) that from the Lord you will receive (*as your inheritance*) the (*same*) reward of the life and immortality (*found in Him*): because you have hearkened to (*being obedient to*) the faith of the Lord Jesus Christ.

25 But (*know also that*) he that (*does not hearken to the faith of the Lord Jesus*) takes the wrong way unto life (*and has gone aside to his own way*) and will (*from that wrong way*) receive the (*only*) reward it can serve him with (*which way perishes in death*), and there is (*not some different way unto life or*) partiality for (*any*) persons (*whether they are Jew, Gentile, bond or free*).

Chapter 4

1 Masters, give to your servants that which is just and equal; knowing that you also have One greater (*in rule and authority*) than you (*your Father*) in heaven (*who has come to serve us all equally with His justice in Christ Jesus our Lord, giving us His life and immortality as an inheritance by Him*).

2 Continue praying (*at all times*) staying alert in prayer and giving thanks to God;

3 And pray also for us, that God would open to us a door for the word, (*so that we may boldly*) declare the mystery of Christ, because of which (*word*) I am also imprisoned:

4 So that I may make the mystery (*of Christ clearly*) known (*to all people, freely*) speaking as I ought to speak.

5 Walk (*abiding*) in the wisdom (*of Christ*) toward those that are without (*having not yet heard or received the word of Christ*), so that you make the most of every opportunity.

6 (*Where you*) allow the words you speak to be filled with (*His*) grace, seasoned with salt (*with the message of Gods righteousness to preserve your life from the death and corruption that is in the world*), so that you might know how you ought to answer every man (*about the hope that is in you*).

7 Tych'i-cus will tell you about all the things concerning me, he is a beloved brother and faithful minister of Christ and fellow helper (*with me*) in the gospel of the Lord:

8 Who I have sent to you for this very purpose, so that you might know the things concerning us and he might encourage your hearts (*in the truth*);

9 (*Along*) with O'nes'i-mus, (*who is also*) a faithful and beloved brother and one of you. They will tell you of all the things that are done here.

10 Ar-is-tar'chus my fellow prisoner greets you as does Mark, who is the cousin of Bar'na-bas, (concerning whom you have received my instructions: that if he comes to you, receive him;)

11 And also Jesus, who is called Jus'tus, who is from the circumcision. These men are (*not only*) my fellow laborers in the kingdom of God, but they have also been a comfort to me.

12 Ep'a-phras, who is one of you, a servant (*who willingly belongs*) to Jesus Christ, greets you, (*who is*) always earnestly contending for you in his prayers, that you may stand perfect and complete in all that God desires for you.

13 Because I bear witness of him, that he has a great care for you, and (*also*) for those that are in La-od-i-ce'a, and in Hi-e-rap'o-lis.

14 Luke, the beloved physician, and Demas, greet you.

15 Greet the brothers that are in Laodicea, along with Nym'phas and all the church that meets in his house.

16 And when this letter is read among you, see to it that it also be read in the church of the La-od-i-ce'ans; and that you also read the letter from La-od-i-ce'a.

17 And say to Ar-chip'pus, take care (*to keep your eyes upon*) the ministry which you have received from the Lord, so that you fulfill it.

18 The greeting in this letter is by the hand of me, Paul. Remember (*me* in) my bonds. Grace be with you. Amen.

The First Epistle of Paul to the

THESSALONIANS

The Faith Translation

Chapter 1

1 Paul, and Silas, and Timothy, to the church of the Thessalonians which is in God the Father and in the Lord Jesus Christ: (*His*) Grace (*and strength*) is unto you, and peace (*that brings rest inside of the unity which comes*) from God our Father, and the Lord Jesus Christ.

2 We give thanks to God (*the Father*) always for you all, making mention of you in our prayers;

3 Remembering without ceasing the work which the faith *has done in you*, even your labor (*which comes*) from the love (*of God for all people*), and the patience (*which is born*) from the hope (*you have*) in our Lord Jesus Christ, (*to stand blameless*) before the God and our Father of us all (*in His love and full of His glory*);

4 Knowing, brethren beloved (*of the Father*), that this is the life chosen of God for you (*from the beginning*).

5 And how that the gospel we preached did not come to you in word only, but (*that same word which was made flesh in Christ Jesus our Lord*) was also (*confirmed in us*) by the power (*of God and His love unfeigned*) and in (*the pouring out of*) the Holy Ghost and in full assurance (*of the truth and the certainty of His life*), even as you saw what sort (*of men*) we became among (*and toward*) you for your sake.

6 And you became followers of (*the same way as*) us, even (*as we were followers*) of the Lord Jesus, having received the word in much (*tribulation and*) affliction, (*you received it*) with joy that comes from the Holy Ghost:

7 So (*much so*) that you (*yourselves*) became examples to all that believed (*upon the Lord Jesus*) in Macedonia and Achaia.

8 Because from (*the joy and the hope that*) you (*have in the midst of tribulation it*) has sounded out (*a loud proclamation, declaring*) the word of the Lord not only in Macedonia and Achaia, but also (*reverberating*) in every place *the work that* the faith has done in you to (*manifest the fruit of*) God (*and His life and peace toward you*) has gone forth all over the world; so (*much so*) that we need not to speak anything.

1 Thessalonians 2

9 For those things alone show us what manner of entering in we had unto your hearts, and how you turned to God from idols (*that had no ability to rescue you from the death and affliction you were experiencing*) to serve (*and be served*) by the living and true God;

10 And to wait (*patiently*) for (*the arrival of*) His Son from heaven, whom He raised from the dead, even Jesus, which delivered us from (*death and*) the wrath to come (*against death in the last day*).

Chapter 2

1 For you yourselves, brethren know that our entrance into your hearts was not in vain (*but has brought forth much fruit*):

2 But after we had previously suffered as you well know being shamefully mistreated at Philippi, we waxed bold in (*the testimony of*) God (*in Christ*) to speak (*confidently*) unto you the gospel of God in the midst of so much conflict.

3 For our exhortation was not from deceit, nor of uncleanness (*or from selfish motives*), nor with any guile (*or trickery*):

4 But just as we were proven by God (*in our own hearts*) to be (*persuaded of and*) entrusted with the gospel, even so we speak; not as pleasing men, but God, who approves (*and confirms His testimony in*) our hearts.

5 For as you know, neither did we at any time use flattering words (*of man's wisdom*), nor a cover for greed (*or covetousness*); God is (*our*) witness:

6 Nor did we seek the glory of men, neither from you, nor of others, when we might have been (*weighty and*) burdensome, (*using our authority*) as the apostles of Christ.

7 But we were gentle (*and light*) among you, even as a nurturing mother cherishes her children:

8 Being so affectionately desirous of you (*and the care of your lives*), we were willing to have imparted unto you, not only the gospel of God, but also (*we poured out*) our very lives, because you were so precious to us.

9 For you remember, brethren, our labor and hardships: how that we worked night and day, so that we would not be (*a*

76

burden, or an expense) chargeable to any of you, we preached unto you the gospel of God (*in Christ*).

10 You are witnesses, and God also, how that in a manner fitting of His life and justice and unblameable (*to all men*) we conducted ourselves among you that believe:

11 As you know how we encouraged and comforted and charged every one of you, as a father does his children,

12 So that you would walk (*in the same way, in a manner*) fitting of God (*the Father, and the life He has set apart for you*), who has called you into (*fellowship with Christ and*) His kingdom and glory.

13 For this reason we also thank God without ceasing, because when you received the word of God which you heard from us, you received it not as the word of men, but as it is in truth, the word (*and the testimony*) of God (*in Christ*), which (*word*) is also (*continually*) effectually (*and powerfully*) working in you that believe.

14 For you, brethren, became followers of (*the way like*) the churches of God in Judaea which are in Christ Jesus: for you also have suffered similar things of your fellow countrymen, even as they have of the Jews:

15 Who have both killed the Lord Jesus, and their own prophets, and have persecuted us; and they do not please God, because they are contrary to (*the way by which*) all men (*might experience His life*):

16 Forbidding (*and hindering*) us to speak to the Gentiles so that they might be saved, always (*desiring*) to fill up (*and be justified in*) their own way and (*corrupt*) wisdom: for the wrath (*and judgement against the way that serves with death*) is come upon them to the uttermost.

17 But we, brethren, being separated from your presence for a short time, but not in our heart, have determined even more abundantly to see your faces (*again*) with great desire.

18 Therefore (*having desired*) we would have come to you one or more times, even I Paul; but (*messengers of*) Satan hindered us.

77

1 Thessalonians 3

19 For what is our hope, or joy, or crown that we may boast (*in the Lord*)? Is it not even you (*being glorified along with us*) in the presence of our Lord Jesus Christ at His coming?

20 For you are (*sharing in*) our (*same*) glory and joy (*both now and at His coming*).

Chapter 3

1 For that reason when we could not wait any longer, we thought it best to be left behind at Athens, alone;

2 And sent Timothy, our brother, and minister of God, and our fellow laborer in the gospel of Christ, to establish you, and to comfort you concerning the faith (*of our Lord Jesus*):

3 So that no man should be moved by the tribulations (*and afflictions that will come*): for you yourselves know that we are destined to encounter (*tribulations in this world*).

4 For indeed, we told you beforehand, when we were with you, that we were about to suffer tribulation; just as it came to pass, as you know.

5 For this reason, when I could not wait any longer, I sent (*Timothy*) to know your faith (*was established*), lest by some means the tempter might have tempted you (*to take up the care for your own life*), and our labor be in vain.

6 But now when Timothy came from you back to us, and brought us the good report of your faith and love (*abounding*), and that you have good remembrance of us always, desiring greatly to see us, as we also are to see you:

7 Therefore, brethren, we were comforted (*and encouraged in the Lord*) concerning you in (*the midst of*) all our affliction and distress by (*seeing what*) the faith (*has done*) in you:

8 For now we live (*in the midst of tribulation being ourselves strengthen by the faith of Jesus Christ*), (*as will you*) if you stand fast in (the faith of the Lord (*Jesus*).

9 For what (*other*) thanks can we render to God for you again, (*in return*) for all the joy by which we joy for your sakes before our God (*and Father who saves us to the uttermost*),

10 Praying exceedingly night and day that we might see your faces (*again*), so that we might perfect anything lacking in your faith?

11 Now God Himself and our Father, and our Lord Jesus Christ, direct our way back to you.

12 And the Lord (*Himself*) make you to increase and abound in love one toward another, and toward all men, even as we do toward you:

13 To the end He may establish your hearts blameless (*and unashamed*) set apart before God (*unto the life He has chosen you for from the beginning*), (*to stand before*) even our Father, at the coming of our Lord Jesus Christ with all those (*His saints*) who have called upon His name.

Chapter 4

1 Furthermore then we urge you, brethren, and encourage you by (*the faith of*) the Lord Jesus, that (*faith*) which you have also (*heard and*) received from us how (*the faith declares the way unto life and immortality by which*) you ought to walk and to please God, so that you would abound more and more (*in the fruit of His life*).

2 For (*that reason*) you (*should*) know (*and consider*) what commandments were given you (*in the faith*) of the Lord Jesus.

3 For (*harkening diligently to*) this (*faith*) is the will of God, (*because it is able to persuade you of*) your sanctification (*from death*), so that you should (*rest in Him and*) abstain from fornication (*with other gods that contain no ability to preserve your lives from perishing in death*):

4 So that everyone of you would know (*and be persuaded*) to possess their dying bodies in (*the certainty of*) sanctification (*from death*) and (*in the way fitting of the*) honor (*and value of the life He set us apart for, even unto immortality in our flesh*);

5 Not in the passionate lust for life (*to preserve our dying bodies with the life*) you can serve yourselves (*which perishes in death*), even as the Gentiles who do not know (*the faith of*

1 Thessalonians 4

God (*wherein He provided the certainty that He will also glorify our bodies with immortality*):

6 So that no man (*transgress or*) go beyond (*the judgment of God*) and defraud his brother in any matter: because concerning such things, the Lord is the avenger of them all, as we also have forewarned you and testified.

7 For God has not called us for uncleanness, but for (*His*) life (*that is undefiled by death which*) He set apart for us (*from the beginning*).

8 Therefore he that despises (*his brother*), does not despise man, but God, (*The One*) who has also (*freely*) given unto us His Holy Spirit.

9 But as concerning brotherly love you do not need that I write unto you: for you yourselves are taught of God to love one another.

10 And indeed you do it toward all the brethren which are in all Macedonia: but we implore you, brethren, that you (*continue harkening to the faith so that you*) increase more and more (*in the fruit of His life*)

11 And that you (*would eagerly desire to*) study to be quiet (*still, in peace and rest before Him*), and to do your own business, and to work with your own hands, as we instructed you;

12 So that you may walk honestly toward them that are without (*Christ*), and so that you may have lack of nothing (*not needing to rely upon men from without*).

13 But I would not want you to be ignorant, brethren, concerning those whose (*bodies are*) asleep (*in the grave but are alive with Christ*), so that you do not sorrow, like others who have no hope (*without Christ in the world*).

14 For if we believe that Jesus died and rose again, even so those also whose (*bodies*) sleep (*in the grave but are alive*) in Jesus will God bring with Him.

15 For this we say unto you by the word of the Lord, that we who are alive and remain (*in the body*) until the coming of the Lord will not prevent those who are (*present with the Lord but absent from the body*) asleep (*in the grave*).

16 For the Lord Jesus Himself shall descend from heaven with a shout, with the voice of the archangel, and with the trump of God: and the dead in Christ shall rise (*from the grave*) first: 17 Then we which are alive and remain (*in the body*) shall (*be changed in the twinkling of an eye and*) be caught up together with them in the clouds, to meet the Lord in the air: and so, shall we ever be with the Lord (*for all the ages to come*). 18 Therefore (*let us*) comfort one another with these words.

Chapter 5

1 Now concerning the times and the seasons, brethren, you have no need that I (*or anyone*) write unto you. 2 For yourselves know perfectly well that the day of the Lord will come in the same manner as a thief in the night. 3 For when they (*who are in darkness*) shall say, Peace and safety; then sudden destruction comes upon them (*startling them like a thief, when the secrets of their hearts are laid bare*), as (*labor and*) travail comes upon a woman with child; and they shall not be able to escape (*the fear in their hearts when their nakedness is exposed, causing them to run unto destruction*). 4 But you, brethren, are not in darkness, that that day should overtake you (*in fear*) as a thief. 5 You are all the children of light (*of His life*), and the children of the day: we are not of the night, nor of darkness. 6 Therefore let us not sleep (*in idleness*), as do others; but let us be (*diligent*) watchful (*sober*) and clear minded. 7 For they that sleep, sleep in the night; and they that be drunken are drunken in the night. 8 But let us, who are of the day (*and of the light*), be sober, putting on the breastplate of faith and love (*by harkening diligently to the faith which guards your heart from fear*), and (*protects your mind*) like an helmet, (*finding rest in*) the (*sure*) hope of salvation (*from death and the likeness of His resurrection*).

1 Thessalonians 5

9 For God has not appointed us to wrath (*or destruction*), but to obtain salvation (*by which our lives are preserved eternally*) by (*the power of*) the Lord Jesus Christ (*indestructible life*),

10 Who died for us (*leaving death in the grave*), so that, whether we are awake (*and remain*) or (*our bodies have fallen*) asleep, (*at His return*), we should all live together with Him (*forever with the same glory and immortality in our flesh*).

11 Wherefore comfort yourselves together, and edify one another (*in the faith*), even as also you do (*yourself*).

12 And we encourage you, brethren, to know (*and communicate with*) them who (*are compelled by the love of God for all people to*) labor (*in the gospel*) among you, and are over you in the Lord (*teaching you in the faith of Jesus Christ*), and correcting you (*as ones who care for your lives as their own*);

13 And to esteem them very highly in love for their work's sake. And be at peace among yourselves (*and with all men*).

14 Now we exhort you, brethren, admonish them that are unruly (*or disorderly*), comfort the faint-hearted (*that they faint not*), support the weak, be patient toward all men.

15 See that no one return evil for evil to any man; but always follow that which is good, both among yourselves, and toward all men.

16 Rejoice (*in His loving-kindness to serve you with His indestructible life and glory*) evermore.

17 Pray (*in all things*) without ceasing (*openly sharing your heart with the Father*).

18 In everything offer thanksgiving (*calling upon the name of the Lord and taking His cup of salvation*): for this is the (*perfect*) will of God (*revealed*) in Christ Jesus concerning you.

19 Do not quench (*or reject*) the Spirit (*of truth speaking to your inner man*).

20 Despise not prophesying's (*divine utterances that provide clarity, understanding and reveal the depths and the mysteries of Christ*).

21 Prove all things (*with the word of truth*); holding fast to that which is good.

22 Withdraw from all appearances of evil (*those things which are filled with harassing labors and hardships that are not born from life*).

23 Now the very God of peace (*Himself has*) sanctified you (*from death with His own blood*) completely (*once and for all time*); so that He may preserve your entire spirit and soul and body blameless (*free from death's accusation*) unto the coming of our Lord Jesus Christ (*and the redemption of your bodies immortal*).

24 Faithful is He that called you (*into fellowship with His Son Jesus Christ our Lord and into union with His life and immortality*), who also will do it.

25 Brethren, pray for us (*that the gospel may have free course and be glorified even as it was with you*).

26 Greet all the brethren with an holy kiss.

27 I charge you (*emphatically*) by the Lord that this epistle be read unto all the holy brethren (*the ones that see they have been set apart for His life*).

28 The grace of our Lord Jesus Christ be with you all. Amen. {The first epistle unto the Thessalonians was written from Athens.

The Second Epistle of Paul to the

THESSALONIANS

The Faith Translation

Chapter 1

1 Paul, and Silas, and Timothy, to the church of the Thessalonians *who are kept* (*from death's accusation*) by God our Father and the Lord Jesus Christ:

2 (*His*) Grace (*and strength*) unto you, and peace, from God our Father and the Lord Jesus Christ.

3 We are compelled to thank God for you always, brethren, as it is fitting (*of thanksgiving*), because the faith (*of Him*) is growing (*and working*) in you exceedingly, and (*has manifested in you*) abundantly in the love every one of you has toward each other;

4 So (*much so*) that we ourselves glory in you in all the churches of God (*around the world*) for your patience and faith in (*the midst of*) all the persecutions and tribulations that you endure (*which are a testimony that gives glory to God*):

5 A visible proof of the righteous judgment of God (*to serve you with all the fruit of His life*), so that you may be seen in (*the exact expression of*) the life (*He*) deemed fitting of the kingdom of God, for which you also (*now*) suffer:

6 If indeed it is a righteous thing with God to recompense affliction to that which afflicts you.

7 And (*give*) to you who are afflicted, rest (*along*) with us, (*then*) when the Lord Jesus shall be revealed from heaven with His mighty angels,

8 In flaming fire (*of His light and life*) taking vengeance (*and delivering justice*) on (*and against the death that afflicted all His beloved including*) them that know not God, and that were disobedient (*refusing to be persuaded*) of the gospel of our Lord Jesus Christ:

9 Who will be (*expecting to be*) punished (*and not rewarded, will to His displeasure run*) with (*fear*) to everlasting destruction from the presence of the Lord, and from the glory of His power;

10 When He shall come to (*glorify and*) be glorified inside of His saints (*those who have called upon the name of the Lord*), and to be marveled among all that believe (*who will be*

awestruck at His glory) [because the testimony (*of Christ*) was believed among you] in that day (*when the Lord comes to glorify His beloved*).

11 Therefore also we pray always for you, that (*you know with certainty that*) God (*our Father*) deemed you worthy of the calling (*of His life and immortality*), and (*He by His strength alone will*) fulfil all the good pleasure of His goodness, and the work of faith (*you have seen and believed in the faith of Jesus Christ*) with power:

12 So that the name of our Lord Jesus Christ may be glorified in you (*formed in your hearts*), and you in Him, according to the grace (*and strength*) of our God and (*Father unto the same life and likeness as*) the Lord Jesus Christ.

Chapter 2

1 But we exhort you, brethren, (*that*) by (*looking to the sure hope of*) the coming of our Lord Jesus Christ, and by our being gathering together (*as One immortal*) to Him,

2 That you are not soon shaken in your mind, or troubled, neither by spirit, nor by word, nor by letter as if (*supposedly*) from us, (*but find rest in the certainty of His life*) as (*you see*) that the day of Christ (*is approaching and*) in sight.

3 Let no man deceive you by any means: for that day will not come, except there first come a departure from the faith (*of Jesus Christ and the truth revealed in Him*), and the man of iniquity (*and lawlessness*) be revealed, the son of perdition (*whose life is born from destruction*);

4 Who opposes (*Christ*) and exalts himself above (*the only true God and*) all that is called God, or that is worshipped (*as God*); so that he (*alone*) might sit as God in the temple (*and the church*) of God, showing himself (*publicly*) that he is God.

5 Do you not remember that, when I was still there with you, I told you about these things?

6 And now you know what withholds (*that day*) that he might be revealed in his time.

7 Because the mystery of iniquity is already working (*lawlessness in the world*): only (*secretly*) until the One who restrains be taken out of the way (*caught up from out of the midst*).

8 And then will the lawlessness (*that is full of iniquity*) be revealed (*openly*), which the Lord Jesus will consume with the breath of His mouth, and (*He*) will (*completely annul and*) abolish (*the last enemy death*) with the brightness of His (*life and glory*) coming (*to gather His beloved and join heaven and earth together immortal*):

9 Even the one whose coming is according to the working (*and doctrines*) of Satan (*that are filled*) with all power and signs and lying wonders,

10 And (*come*) with every deception that works unrighteousness (*and injustice*) in (*the hearts of*) them that perish because they have rejected (*and have exchanged*) the love of the truth (*for a lie*), so that they might be saved (*from all the injustice of iniquity and death*).

11 And for this reason (*they perish because*) God (*has judged that iniquity*) will send them strong delusion, so that they should believe a lie:

12 And so that (*iniquity would be revealed and judged as the thing that brings the death and condemnation to the hearts of*) all those who believed not the truth but had pleasure in (*iniquity which serves them with the*) injustice (*of perishing in the second death*).

13 But we are bound (*and grateful*) to render thanksgiving always to God for you, brethren beloved of the Lord, because (*this is the life which*) God has chosen for you from the beginning unto salvation (*from death*) through the sanctification of the Spirit (*of life*) and belief of the truth (*through the faith of Jesus Christ*):

14 To this life has He also called you through our gospel, unto the obtaining of the (*same*) glory (*and immortality*) of our Lord Jesus Christ.

15 Therefore, brethren, stand firm (*in the faith of Christ Jesus*), and hold fast to the things we have passed on to you (*which*

we have received from the Lord) which you have been taught (*by us*), whether by word, or our epistle.

16 Now the Lord Jesus Christ Himself, and God, the Father of us all, who has loved us, and has given us everlasting consolation and (*the*) good (*and the sure*) hope (*to appear in the likeness of His life*) through (*His*) grace (*and strength*),

17 May He comfort (*and encourage*) your heart and firmly establish you with every good word and (*good*) work (*which He has done*).

Chapter 3

1 Finally, brethren, pray for us, that the word of the Lord (*that we preach, the gospel of Jesus Christ and Him crucified*) may spread quickly (*throughout the world without hinderance*), and be glorified, just as it is in you:

2 And that we may be delivered from (*the dangers of*) unreasonable and malicious men (*full of iniquity*): for not all men have the faith.

3 But the Lord is faithful, (*being both the One*) who will establish you, (*and who will also strengthen*) and guard *your heart* from evil.

4 And (*for that reason*) we are (*persuaded and*) confident in the (*word of the*) Lord concerning you, that (*the faith works in*) you, to (*both*) do and bring about the things which we (*came along side and*) charged you (*of the Lord*).

5 And the Lord (*will*) direct your hearts (*bringing you*) into the love of God, and into (*rest and*) the patient waiting for Christ.

6 Now we charge you, brethren, in the name of our Lord Jesus Christ, that you withdraw yourselves from every brother that walks disorderly, and not after the ways which we passed on to you which he (*also*) received of us.

7 For yourselves know how you ought to (*walk and*) follow our example: for we did not conduct ourselves disorderly among you;

8 Neither did we eat any man's bread without paying for it; but we worked with labor and hardship night and day, so that we might not be an expense to any of you:

9 Not because we do not have the authority (*to do as we please*), but to make ourselves an example for you to follow us.

10 For even when we were with you, this we commanded you, that if any would not work, neither should he eat (*another man's bread*).

11 For we hear that there are some which walk disorderly among you, (*and are idle*) not working at all but are busybodies (*busy with what others are doing*).

12 Now to them that are doing such things we charge and exhort by our Lord Jesus Christ, that in quietness (*and peacefulness*) they (*do their own*) work and eat their own bread.

13 But you, brethren, (*who diligently harken to the faith*) will not grow weary in doing well (*regardless of what others do*).

14 And if any man does not obey our word by this epistle, note that man, and have no (*intimate*) association with him, so that he may turn away from such things.

15 Yet do not esteem him as an enemy but admonish him as a brother.

16 Now the Lord of peace Himself give you (*His*) peace in every way. The Lord is with you always.

17 The salutation of Paul is written with my own hand, which is the token of every epistle: so, I Paul write:

18 The grace of our Lord Jesus Christ be with you all. Amen. {The second epistle to the Thessalonians was written from Athens.}

The First Epistle of Paul to the

TIMOTHY

The Faith Translation

Chapter 1

1 Paul, (*called to be*) an apostle of Jesus Christ according to the command of God the Savior, and (*the gospel of*) our Lord Jesus Christ (*which was committed to me*), which is the certain hope of (*His life in*) us;

2 To Timothy, my true son in the faith: (*May the*) Grace, mercy, and peace, (*that has come*) from God our Father and Jesus Christ our Lord (*be with you*).

3 Just like I urged you to remain in Eph'e-sus when I was going on to Mac-e-do'ni-a, so that you might warn certain men not to teach any other doctrines (*other than Christ crucified, which I have clearly set forth among them*),

4 Neither give regard (*or devote any attention*) to any (*Jewish*) fables and endless genealogies (*according to the flesh*), which (*contain no power to minster His life but*) only serve to bring about meaningless (*speculation*) questions (*and debate*), rather than godly edifying which is (*only found*) in the faith (*of Jesus Christ*): so (*continue to*) do (*the same everywhere you go*).

5 Now the end of the commandment (*that was from the beginning*) is love (*that flows*) out of a pure heart (*which is one that sees the Father has only ever desired to serve you with His life, where you lack no good thing*), and from a good conscience (*persuaded that He who promised is also able to preserve your lives unto immortality in your flesh*), which is undisguised (*and put on full display*) in the faith (*of Jesus Christ*).

6 From which some, having swerved (*from the faith, have missed the mark*) and turned aside instead to meaningless discourse;

7 Desiring to be teachers of the law, although they are without any understanding about what they say or the things they (*confidently*) assert.

8 But we know that the law is good as long as one makes use of it (*according to the spirit and truth contained in it*) lawfully (*and not lawlessly through the carnal mind*),

9 Knowing this, that the law is not (*and was not*) made for a righteous man (*who has ceased from his own work seeing the*

1 Timothy 1

Father's work is sufficient and able to serve him with His life and immortality), but rather for the lawless (*who transgress the law by seeking to obtain that life through the works of their own hands*) and the disobedient (*who refuse to be persuaded by the work which God has done in Christ Jesus*), for the ungodly and for those laboring to preserve their own life, for unholy and profane (*that are experiencing the fruit of death*), for murderers of fathers and murderers of mothers, and murderers of all men,

10 For fornicators, for them that defile themselves with (*idolatry, seeking the pleasures they can obtain from*) mankind, for (*kidnappers and*) slave owners, for liars, for perjured persons (*who swears falsely against another*), and if there be any other thing that (*brings forth the fruit of death and*) is contrary to sound doctrine (*for those who are without understanding and are still ignorant that the word contained in the law spoke of God's righteousness toward them, to provide Himself the lamb that would cleanse them from death*);

11 (*Which word is*) according to (*the same spirit and truth of*) the glorious gospel of the blessed God, which was committed to my trust.

12 And I am filled with thankfulness (*giving all glory*) to Christ Jesus our Lord, the One who strengthens me, because He has considered me a trustworthy messenger (*of the faith, grace, and love of God for all people*), (*in that He appointed me*) putting me into the ministry;

13 Who was formerly one that spoke slanderously and abusively (*against those of the faith*) and was a persecutor (*that hunted them down*) with intent to injury (*them with violence*): but I found (*that the Father was filled with*) mercy (*toward me*), because I did these things being ignorant (*of the truth*) in unbelief.

14 Then (*the scales fell from my eyes when*) the grace (*and kindness*) of our Lord super abounded (*toward me*) with the faith and love that are found in Christ Jesus.

15 Trustworthy (*and free from any doubt*) is the saying that is filled (*with the faith that came from the Father's heart*) full of

all approval, that Christ Jesus came into the world to save those who were perishing and missing the mark (*the Father had set for their lives of His life and immortality in their flesh, who being filled with lust to produce the fruit of God's life by their own works, instead brought forth the fruit of death and every evil work*); of whom I (*being once filled with that lust*) was the chief.

16 But for this reason was I shown (*to have received His*) mercy so that in me, (*who was*) the chief, Jesus Christ might show forth (*His*) perfect patience as an example for those who would hereafter (*see His mercy and long suffering toward them and*) believe on Him to a life without end.

17 Now unto (*Christ Jesus*) the King (*of glory*) the eternal immortal One, (*in Whom dwells the fullness of the Father*) the invisible and only God, be all honor and glory forever and ever. Amen.

18 This charge (*that no one preach any other doctrine, but Christ crucified, which*) I have committed to you, Timothy, my son (*in the faith*), is according to the prophecies which have gone before you (*and I*), so that through (*the truth contained in*) those prophecies, you might wage a good warfare (*against every false doctrine*);

19 Holding the faith (*of Christ, who is the head which contains all the nourishment*), and (*brings forth*) a good conscience (*toward God*), which some having (*willfully rejected and*) thrust it away (*from themselves*) have made a shipwreck concerning the faith:

20 Among whom are Hymenaeus and Alexander; who I have given over to (*the persuasion in their own hearts and to the fruit that the doctrine of*) Satan (*and his demons serves them*), so that they might learn (*firsthand*) not to speak abusively against (*rejecting the faith as*) the way that leads to (*an incorruptible*) life (*forever free from the sting of death, seeing their persuasion only serves them with the fruit of death*).

Chapter 2

1 I urge you therefore, that first of all, petitions, prayers, intercession, and thanksgiving are made on behalf of all men.
2 For kings and all those that are in authority; that we may lead a quiet and peaceful life giving all reverence and (*glory, and*) honor (*to God as Father, the One who serves us His life*).
3 Because this is good, (*and beautiful*) and acceptable (*and a praiseworthy thing*) in the sight of God our Savior (*and deliverer*);
4 (*The Father of all*) Who desires for all men to be saved (*from perishing in death*) and come to the knowledge of the truth.
5 Seeing as there is one God (*and Father who is able to serve us with an incorruptible life*), and one mediator between God and men (*who came from the heart of the Father, born of a woman, born of the Spirit*), the man Christ Jesus;
6 Who in the fullness of time, gave Himself a ransom for all (*men*), and became the testimony of (*the Father about*) all (*men*).
7 It is in regard to that (*testimony that*) I was appointed a preacher, an apostle (*to all men*), (I speak the truth in Christ and do not lie;) a teacher of the Gentiles pertaining to the faith (*of Jesus Christ*) and (*the grace of God in*) truth.
8 I desire therefore that all men pray everywhere (*calling upon the name of the Lord*), lifting up holy hands (*in reverential awe of the One who can preserve their lives forever from death and corruption*) apart from (*the fear of*) wrath and doubt (*an inner reasoning that they could preserve their own lives*).
9 And (*I also desire*) that in the same way a women would adorn themselves with modest apparel, so also (*would I that they be decorated*) with self-control and soundness of mind, and not with (*pride from outward appearances like*) braided hair, or gold, pearls or costly clothing;
10 But (*from a heart filled with*) the way that is fitting for a woman professing the (*promise of His*) life and Godlikeness (*standing in silence and*) with (*reverential awe of His*) good works (*to adorn them with all the fruit of His life*).

11 So let the woman learn (*of Him*) in (*humility and*) silence, (*peace and reverential awe*) with all obedience (*and submission to the faith*).

12 However, do not permit a woman (*that has not yet submitted themselves to the faith of Jesus Christ*) to teach (*or exert control or influence over*) any man but to (*let her first*) learn in (*humility and*) silence (*at the feet of Jesus*).

13 For Adam was formed first, then Eve (*because the man is not of the woman; but the woman of the man*).

14 And Adam was not deceived (*by the serpent*), but the woman having already been deceived (*exerted her influence over Adam to partake and they*) fell into the transgression.

15 Nevertheless they are saved through the woman bearing (*the promised seed that crushed the serpents head*) if they abide in the faith of Christ and (*His*) love unto the same life and immortality they were always set apart for with (*peace and*) soundness of mind.

Chapter 3

1 Faithful (*and true*) is this saying: If anyone aspires to be an overseer (*that watches over the cares and concerns of the household of God*), he desires a good work.

2 It behooves the overseer to be above reproach, the husband of one wife, sound minded, self-controlled, respectable, hospitable (*to strangers*), and able to teach (*the faith*),

3 Not inclined to (*the abuse of*) wine (*or strong drink*), not contentious but gentle and peaceful, not greedy for gain or the lover of money,

4 One that cares for his own house well, whose children are not riotous or disobedient with all dignity,

5 (Because if one does not know how to care well for their own house, how will they care for the church of God?)

6 They should not be a new convert, so as not to find themselves lifted up with pride (*in their heart*) where they fall into the condemnation of (*judging themselves according to the flesh which is the wisdom of*) the accuser (*the devil*).

1 Timothy 3

7 Now also it behooves them to have a good testimony from those outside (*the church*) so that they do not fall into reproach (*and are caught in an accusation*) by the snare of (*those animated by death, which is the device*) the devil (*uses*).

8 Deacons likewise must not be deceitful or an abuser of wine (*or strong drink*), not given to greed, the love of money or dishonest gain,

9 Holding the mystery (*of the gospel*) contained in the faith (*of the Son of God*) with a pure heart (*and conscience toward God the Father to serve them with His incorruptible life*).

10 Also let these things first be proven; then allow them serve (*as a deacon*) being blameless (*free from accusation*).

11 And their wives likewise should be dignified and not a false accuser, clear-minded, trustworthy in all things.

12 Let the deacons be the husbands of one wife, that care well for their children and their own household.

13 For those who (*desire to*) serve excellently, as a deacon obtain to (*and stand as*) a good influence (*to the church body*), and (*do so*) with great boldness in the faith which is in Christ Jesus (*our Lord*).

14 These things I write to you, but I am hoping to come to you shortly:

15 But if it takes longer than expected, (*I am writing*) so that you might know how to conduct yourself in the house of God, which is (*His body*) the church of the living God, the pillar (*of support*) and foundation of the truth (*in Christ*).

16 And apart from any and all dispute, great (*and filled with the most stunning awe and amazement one could ever experience*) is the mystery (*of all the ages*), of Godliness (*Godlikeness inside human flesh, wherein the everlasting kindness and love of God was revealed in*) the righteous act of (*the only true*) God (*the only immortal*) to serve us with His life (*and immortality*): that He was manifest inside of dying (*human*) flesh, (*by which He, the just and the justifier*) justified (*all men from the accusation that dying flesh was not a word they were not the children of God, by standing up from the grave in incorruptible flesh and ascending in that flesh higher*

than the heavens) through the Spirit, seen of angels, preached among the nations, (*to the fatherless, the stranger and the widow*), believed on in the world, and received up into glory (*on the right hand of the Majesty on high*).

Chapter 4

1 But the Spirit speaks expressly (*without any ambiguity*), that in the latter times some (*who having been misled*) will depart from the faith (*of Jesus Christ and Him crucified*), giving heed (*instead*) to (deceptive and) seducing spirits, and (*ear tickling teachings and*) doctrines that come from demons (*having a form of Godliness but denying the true Godliness which is the only thing that ever had the power to destroy death in the flesh unto immortality*),

2 Speaking (*the same*) lies (*as the serpent, they appear clean on the outside but inside are filled*) with hypocrisy (*and the deadly poison of asps which is iniquity*); having their (*heart and*) conscience (*marked by the beast as if*) seared with a hot (*branding*) iron,

3 Forbidding to marry (*as if doing so could make one unclean, when in fact God gave marriage as a token sign of His desire to be One flesh with us*) and commanding others to abstain from meats (*of flesh that they have deemed as unclean*), which (*flesh*) God has created to be received with thanksgiving by them which believe and know the truth.

4 For every creature of God is good (*and acceptable*), and nothing is to be rejected, if it is received with thanksgiving:

5 Because it has been sanctified (*as clean and undefiled*) by the word which God has spoken (*in Christ*) and (*by His*) intercession (*in our hearts*).

6 If you remind the brethren of these things, you will be a good minister of (*the faith of*) Jesus Christ, nourished up (*and persuaded*) by the word of faith and from the good sound doctrine (*it imparts*), which (*teaching*) you know (*and understand well having kept it close to your heart*).

97

1 Timothy 4

7 But refuse *(to have anything to do with)* profane *(teachings of the principles of the world like touch not, taste not, handle not)* and old wives' tales *(that cross over the threshold of sound doctrine)*, but rather exercise yourself unto *(true)* Godliness *(which is the work which God has done to serve you with His life and Godlikeness in your flesh)*.

8 For bodily exercise profits *(very)* little *(and then fades away)*: but Godliness is profitable unto all things *(pertaining to His incorruptible life and Godlikeness)*, containing the promise of the *(Spirit of)* life that has come and now is, and of that which is to come *(in our flesh being made immortal in the new heaven and new earth)*.

9 This is a trustworthy saying that is filled *(with the faith that came from the Father's heart in Jesus Christ and is)* full of all *(His)* approval.

10 For this reason therefore do we both *(diligently)* labor *(contending for the faith)* and suffer reproach *(from preaching the truth of the gospel)*, because we have set our hope *(only)* in the living God, who is the Savior of all men, especially of those that believe *(and find strength and rest from the hope and the promise of eternal life made immortal flesh)*.

11 These things declare and teach.

12 Let no man despise *(or deem you unqualified because of)* your youthful age; but be an example for all the believers, in your teaching *(and in the reasoning of your speech)*, in the manner of your life, by *(abiding in the)* love *(of God for all people)*, in *(declaring)* the faith, in purity *(and without mixed motives)*.

13 Until I come, attend the public readings *(of the scripture)* to encourage and to teaching *(concerning the truth)*.

14 Do not neglect *(or disregard)* the gift that is in you *(but continue to kindle the flames)* of that which was delivered to you *(by the Holy Spirit)* by prophecy, with the laying on of my hands *(in the presence of the elders of the church)*.

15 *(Be diligent to think, consider and)* meditate upon these things; give yourself fully to them; so that your advancement *(of the gospel)* would appear before all *(men)*.

16 Give close attention to yourself (*first*) and (*then*) to the doctrine (*that you teach others, so that you be in the faith*), and continue in it: for in doing this you will both rescue yourself, as well as those that hear you (*from the death and corruption in the world unto a lively hope*).

Chapter 5

1 Do not (*strike back at or*) speak with harsh words to an elder, but encourage (*exhort and comfort, treating*) him as you would your own father and the younger men as brothers,

2 And the elder women (*treat*) as mothers; the younger as sisters, with all purity (*of heart*).

3 Honor widows that are truly widows.

4 But if any widow has children, grandchildren, or family at home allow them first to learn to honor them (*giving reverence to whom reverence is due*), by returning the same (*love and*) care for their parents (*that their parents gave to them*): for that is good and acceptable to God (*fitting of the faith that is in the Father's heart*).

5 Now she who is truly a widow is bereaved and alone, whose hope is in God, and she continues in requests and prayers night and day.

6 But (*not*) she who (*is married to the world and*) lives in (*self-indulgence and worldly*) pleasure (*which actually only looks like life in its outward appearance but inside she*) is dead even while she lives (*seeing as the world has no life to offer*).

7 And declare these truths (*confidently*) so that all may be without blame.

8 But if anyone (*in the church gives no thought and*) has no regard (*in their heart*) for (*the welfare of*) his own family, especially for those of his own house (*that which even the heathens need not be commanded*), he has rejected (*and is not persuaded of*) the faith (*that is in the Father's heart for him*) and (*the persuasion in his heart*) is worse than an unbeliever.

9 Let none be listed as widows, that are under sixty years of age, but rather have been the wife of one man,

10 Well testified of for her good works; if she has brought up children, if she has lodged strangers, if she has washed the saints' feet, if she has given relief to the afflicted, if she has (*not refused but*) diligently followed every good (*and beautiful*) work (*when given the opportunity to do so*).

11 But the younger widows decline: because whenever they grow desirous for sensual pleasures (*in the world*) they wander away from Christ, and will marry,

12 Holding a judgment of themselves (*in their hearts*) because they have set aside their first (*love and*) confidence in Christ.

13 And whereby (*casting away their dependence on Christ*) they learn to be lazy (*and unprofitable*) wandering from house to house; and not only lazy but gossipers (*and taking part in foolish babbling*) also meddling in the affairs of others, speaking things which they ought not to speak.

14 I would rather therefore that a younger woman marries and bears children, keeps watch over her household, where (*in doing so*) they give no occasion for the adversary to speak against them (*and bring condemnation to their heart*).

15 For some are already turned (*wandering from Christ*) back to Satan (*the accuser*).

16 If any (*man or*) woman (*who are of the household*) of faith have a widow (*that is a close relative*), let them help (*and care for*) them and do not burden the church with it, so that it may (*focus on and*) provide relief for them that are truly widows.

17 Let the elders that serves excellently (*over the church*) be deemed fitting of double honor, particularly those who (*also*) labor in the word and the doctrine (*of Christ crucified*).

18 Because the scripture says, you should not muzzle an ox that is treading out grain. And (*so also*) the (*elder*) laborer is considered worthy of his reward (*of double honor*).

19 Do not accept an accusation against an elder, except if (*it can be established*) upon two or three witnesses.

20 But those that have committed offenses correct openly (*with the truth*) so that others also may (*see your faith and*) revere (*God*).

21 I testify to you in the sight of God, and the Lord Jesus Christ, and the elect messenger, (*charging*) that you oversee these things without preferring one man over another, doing nothing by partiality (*or respect of persons*).

22 Do not lay hands quickly on any man (*that rejects correction*), (*whereby you*) neither share in (*fellowship with or contribute to*) other men's iniquity: keep yourself pure.

23 Drink no longer (*only*) water (*being totally abstinent*) but use a little wine for your stomach's sake and your frequent infirmities (*so others may see that is not what defiles a man*).

24 The fruit of death can often be plainly seen in some men's errors (*which are*) foretelling the judgment (*of what that iniquity will produce*); and some men's (*are hid for a time but of a certainty the end of those things*) will be revealed later.

25 Likewise also the good works of some are plainly seen beforehand (*displaying the fruit which the Spirit will produce*); and they that are not (*at first*) seen openly cannot be hid (*but of a certainty will produce the fruit of righteousness unto immortality in the flesh*).

Chapter 6

1 Let all that are under a yoke of a servant esteem their own (*earthly*) masters (*or those who rule over you*) worthy of all honor so that the name of God and His doctrine be not (*defamed or*) spoken evil of.

2 And those (*servants*) that have believing masters, let them not look down upon (*despising them*), because they are also brethren; but rather serve them (*well*), because they are believing and beloved partakers (*along with you*) that have grabbed hold of the (*same*) benefit (*in Christ as you*). These things teach and exhort.

3 If any man teaches another (*contrary*) doctrine that does not agree with the pure words (*of sound doctrine*), even (*rejecting*) the words of our Lord Jesus Christ and the faith which is (*the doctrine that brings forth all the fruit of His life in us*) unto Godlikeness (*in our flesh*);

1 Timothy 6

4 He is puffed up (*and full of pride*), knowing nothing, but having an unhealthy affection for (*foolish*) questions and (*unprofitable*) disputes over words, from out of which comes envy, contention, and every evil, malicious (*laborious and pain-ridden thought and*) imagination,

5 And perverse disputing from men with (*carnal*) minds (*proceeding from hearts*) corrupted (*by death*), and destitute of the truth, supposing that to gain (*a good life by gathering the corruptible things of this world to themselves*) is Godliness: from such (*nonsensical teaching and disputing*) withdraw yourself.

6 But (*rather rest in the One who has promised to serve you with all things pertaining to His life and*) Godlikeness (*in your flesh immortal*) which (*hope is the thing that*) brings true contentment (*to your heart and*) is great gain.

7 For we brought nothing into this world, and it is a certainty that we can carry nothing out of it (*for all the things we could gather, which this world can produce, are perishable*).

8 And (*being persuaded by the faith of Jesus Christ that is unto Godlikeness in our flesh immortal and which clothes us in the fruit of His life*) this (*faith*) allows us (*to rest in our hearts and minds and therein*) having food and clothing to be content (*fully satisfied by His life and the sure hope of the same glory to be revealed in us*).

9 But they that desire to be rich fall into a temptation which is a snare (*to run after the corruptible things of this world*), and into many foolish and hurtful lusts, which (*never satisfy but*) plunge men into ruin and destruction.

10 For the love of money is the root of all evil (*that serves a man with labors, annoyances, hardships and every grievous unjust work*): wherein some that longed after have erred (*and been seduced and overtaken and have thereby strayed away*) from the faith (*of Jesus Christ*), and they have pierced themselves through with many sorrows.

11 But you, O man (*born*) of God, run from these things; and pursue the life and immortality the Father serves you with in

Christ Jesus which is unto Godlikeness (*in your flesh*), (*and the fruit the Spirit bears;*) faith, love, patience, meekness.

12 Fight the good fight (*running the race set before you by never turning away*) from the faith, laying hold on eternal life, (*the life*) unto which He has also called you (*from the beginning*), and which you have confessed the good confession (*of the faith*) before many witnesses.

13 I give you this charge in the sight of God, who (*quickens the dead and*) gives life to all things, and before Christ Jesus, the One that testified before Pontius Pilate the good confession (*that He was indeed Christ, the King*);

14 So that (*abiding in Him*) you keep (*and are kept by*) the commandment, spotless, (*pure and undefiled from death's accusation*), blameless, until the appearing of our Lord Jesus Christ:

15 Who in the fullness of time when He will return, will reveal (*Himself*), (*the One*) Who is the blessed and only true (*Potentate*) Ruler, the King of kings, and Lord of lords (*who lives and reigns in the power of an endless life and of whose kingdom there is no end*);

16 The One Who alone possesses (*the power and dominion to serve men with*) immortality, dwelling in the light (*and life, the full expression and glory of the Godhead bodily, which glory is*) unapproachable (*through the strength of a man's hands*); whom no man has seen, nor can see (*but by the revelation of Jesus Christ*): to whom be all honor and power everlasting. Amen.

17 Instruct those that are rich in this present world, (*charging them*) that they should not be prideful (*and look down upon others of lower estate*) nor place their hope in the uncertainty of riches, but in the (*certainty of the*) living God (*to serve them with His life and immortality*), the One who supplies us (*the only life our hearts have ever truly desired*) abundantly (*where we find contentment that we lack no good thing, and being free from lust, we can simply enjoy*) everything (*created*) for our enjoyment;

1 Timothy 6

18 So that (*in looking to the abundance of His life and the certainty they lack no good thing*) it would work that which is good (*in their hearts*), and wherein they will be rich in (*the abundance of His supply and*) good works, and (*thereby filled with*) the generosity to distribute, and the willingness to share;

19 Laying up (*in abundance and storing away*) for themselves (*treasures that unlike those in the present world cannot ever see corruption, having*) a good foundation (*in their heart*) so that in the time to come, they may lay hold on that which is truly (*His incorruptible*) life.

20 O Timothy, (*above all things guard your heart and be established in and*) keep (*on hearing the faith*) that which is committed to your trust, (*discerning and*) avoiding profane and worthless babbling, and arguments which are falsely called (*wisdom, special*) knowledge (*or sound doctrine*):

21 Which some professing (*their trust in these strange doctrines*) have erred concerning the faith (*of Jesus Christ*). Grace be with you. Amen.

The Second Epistle of Paul to the

TIMOTHY

The Faith Translation

Chapter 1

1 Paul, an apostle of Jesus Christ by the will of God, according to the promise (*that was from the beginning*) of His life (*which promise was made immortal flesh*) in Christ Jesus our Lord.

2 To Timothy, my beloved son: grace, mercy and peace that comes from God the Father and Christ Jesus our Lord.

3 I am thankful to God, whom I serve from my ancestors with a pure conscience (*filled with His goodness and desire toward me to serve me with His life*), (*for your genuine and unconcealed faith*), that without ceasing I have remembrance of you in my prayer's night and day;

4 Longing to see you, remembering your tears (*when I departed*), so that I may be filled with joy (*upon seeing you again*);

5 When I call to remembrance the sincere faith that is born in you (*undisguised and free from hypocrisy*), which (*faith*) first dwelt in your grandmother Lois, and your mother Eunice; I am persuaded that it dwells in you also.

6 Therefore I put you in remembrance (*unceasingly*) that you might stir up (*kindling the flames of*) the gift from (*the Spirit of*) God that is in you, from the laying on of my hands.

7 For God has not given us the spirit of cowardice (*and fearfulness*) but of (*boldness, that His Spirit in us is the*) power (*that even overcomes the death in our flesh*) and of love (*in that He laid down His life for us so that He might raise us up with Him*) and of self-control (*which is a sound mind that rests in His strength to overcome all things and not our own*).

8 Therefore you do not need to be ashamed of the testimony of our Lord, or of me a prisoner (*for His sake*): but a partaker of the afflictions of the gospel according to the (*true*) power (*and strength behind your life, which is the Spirit*) of (*the living*) God (*where you do not need to enlist your own strength and ability to preserve your life*);

9 Who has saved us (*from death*), and called us with an holy calling (*setting us apart for the only life He ever saw fitting for His children, to appear in the likeness of His life and immortality*), not according to our works, but according to His

own purpose and grace, which was (*promised and*) given us in Christ Jesus before the world began (*before death entered*),

10 But is now made manifest (*in flesh in the resurrection*) by the appearing of our Savior Jesus Christ, who has abolished death (*in the flesh*), and has brought life and immortality to light (*shining upon our hearts*) through the glorious gospel (*of the glory of God in the face of Jesus Christ*):

11 To which (*gospel*) I am appointed (*and compelled*) to declare (*to all people*), as an apostle, and a teacher (*of the Gentiles*).

12 For the sake of the gospel I also suffer these afflictions, but I am not ashamed because I know (*the One*) whom I have believed (*whose testimony overcomes the death in the world*) and (*therefore*) I am persuaded that He is able to keep (*me and*) that which He has committed to me unto the day (*of the Lord*).

13 Grab hold of (*the faith and continue hearing*) the (*only*) form of sound words (*and doctrine*), which you have heard from me (*and which are able to keep you*) in the faith and the love that is only found in Christ Jesus (*our Lord*).

14 And that good thing which was committed to you (*will*) keep (*you*) by the Holy Ghost which dwells in us.

15 Know this, that all in Asia have turned away from (*the persecution that comes from association with*) me (*and the gospel I declare*), among whom are Phy-gel'lus and Her-mog'e-nes.

16 The Lord give mercy to the house of On-e-siph'o-rus; for he has often refreshed (*and comforted*) me, and was not ashamed (*of the gospel or*) of my chains (*for its sake*):

17 To the extent that when he was in Rome, he sought me out very diligently, and found me.

18 The Lord gives (*mercy*) to him so that he may (*know and*) find mercy (*in the face*) of the Lord (*Jesus Christ*) in that day (*of His coming*): and about the many things he ministered to me at Eph'e-sus, you know very well.

Chapter 2

1 Therefore you, my son, be strengthened with the grace (*and strength*) that is (*found*) in Christ Jesus (*and not your own*).

2 Timothy 2

2 And the things which you have heard (*declared*) from me in the presence of many witnesses, this same (*grace and faith*) set before faithful men (*for deposit*), who will then be able to teach others.

3 And thereby you share in (*His*) suffering (*along with me*), as a good soldier of Christ Jesus.

4 No man that serves as a soldier (*of Christ*) entangles himself in the affairs of this life (*that is perishing*); so that he may please the One who has chosen him to serve as a soldier (*who partakes in His incorruptible life*).

5 And if a man also competes in a race, he is not crowned unless he competes lawfully.

6 (*So also it was fitting that Christ*) the master gardener that labored must be the first partaker of the fruits.

7 Consider what I say, and the Lord will give you understanding in all things.

8 Remember that Jesus Christ (*a descendant*) of the seed of David was raised from the dead according to my gospel (*which is not according to man's reasoning but Christ*):

9 Wherein I suffer hardship, (*and stand accused*) as an evil doer, even unto imprisonment; but the word of God (*in Christ in me*) is not bound.

10 Therefore I (*am strengthened to*) endure all things (*through Christ and*) for (*Him*) the elect sake (*so I may stand as an example to those who will hereafter believe*) so that they might also (*look to His strength and*) obtain the salvation which is in Christ Jesus in eternal glory.

11 This is a faithful saying (*of which we can be certain*): For if we be dead with Him (*to the corruptible life in this world*), we shall also live with Him (*in the power of His endless life and bodily immortality*):

12 Because if we suffer (*with Him, being made conformable to the death that He died unto the world*), we will also reign with Him (*in the power of His endless life*): if we deny (*and reject*) Him (*and the life He has always desired to serve us with, for the life we can serve ourselves in the world*), He will deny (*that*

way has any ability to serve) us (with His life but only with destruction):

13 If we (refuse to be persuaded and) believe not, yet He abides (forever) faithful (and true): (for) He cannot deny Himself (as the only One who is able to serve us with His life that lives and abides forever immortal).

14 Of these things (continually) remind them, clearly laying out the testimony of the Lord, so that they will not argue about words which (arguments) have no profit but to (the destruction and) overthrow of the hearers.

15 With all diligence (study, giving your full attention to the faith so that you continually) show yourself (the testimony that has been fully scrutinized and) approved by God (not to justify yourself before men), a laborer that does not need to be ashamed (of the gospel), rightly (and accurately) dividing the word of truth (that profits unto eternal life).

16 But avoid blasphemous (illegitimate) and worthless arguments (that stand opposed to the faith of Jesus Christ): for they will only lead to more ungodliness (which is irreverence and disregard for the work of God in Christ).

17 And the word of the ungodly (and irreverent) will eat (and spread) like gangrene: among whom is (the word of) Hy-me-nae'ous and Phi-le-tus;

18 Who concerning the (word of) truth have erred, saying the resurrection (of the dead) is past already (destroying the hope) and overthrowing the faith of some (of the hearers).

19 Nevertheless the foundation of God (in Christ) stands sure, having this seal (and the certainty that His testimony provides), that the Lord knows those that are His (who have called upon His name). And so that (being persuaded of the hope and certainty of His life) everyone that names the name of Christ (will) depart from iniquity (and find rest from the labor to preserve their own life).

20 But in a great house there are both vessels of gold and silver (who have called upon the name of the Lord) but also those of wood and of earth (who look to satisfy themselves with

2 Timothy 2

the corruptible things of the world); some unto honor and some unto dishonor.

21 If any man (*looks to the faith that came from the heart of the Father in Christ he will*) purge himself from these (*things that cannot ever serve him with honor but only with dishonor*), he will be a vessel unto honor, sanctified (*from death*) and profitable to (*the satisfaction of*) the master's will (*and desire, which has always been to serve with His incorruptible life*), and prepared to (*walk in*) every good work (*which the Father has set apart for him*).

22 (*Therefore*) flee also from youthful lusts (*to satisfy yourself and your desire for life*): but rather follow righteousness, (*looking unto Jesus to fill that desire, where you allow Him to serve you with that life of*) faith, love, and peace, (*along*) with those that call on the name of the Lord out of a pure heart (*and thereby receive honor from the Father*).

23 But foolish and ignorant questions (*and meaningless debate and speculation*) avoid, knowing that they do give birth to (*contention and*) quarrels.

24 And the one who serves (*the word of*) the Lord has no need to be quarrelsome (*or contentious*) but gentle toward all men, able to teach, enduring (*persecution*) patiently,

25 In humility instructing (*and correcting with the word of truth*) those (*whose hearts stand*) opposed to themselves (*obtaining the life they truly desire*), so that when (*they see the work of*) God (*in Christ, He is the one that*) will (*persuade their heart and*) give them a change in their minds (*that destroys every opposition and brings repentance*) unto the acknowledging of the truth;

26 And so that (*by hearing the faith of Jesus Christ*) they may regain their senses (*and sound mind*) where they are able to be set free from the snare of (*death's accusation which had all their lifetime held them captive to the fear of death which came from that slanderous accuser*) the devil, those who (*not being persuaded of the faith*) are taken captive by him at his will.

Chapter 3

1 Know this also, that during these last days (*of death in the earth*) there will come perilous (*dangerous*) times (*hard to bear*).

2 Because men will be lovers of themselves (*and the life they can gather to themselves in the world*) covetous (*lovers of money*), boasters (*that make empty claims*), proud (*and lifted up in their own hearts*), blasphemers (*who claim godliness but slander God's name*), (*children will be*) disobedient to parents, ungrateful, unholy (*without reverence for what God has set apart*),

3 Without natural affection (*callous and unloving*), unsatisfied (*and disagreeable*), false accusers (*that speak the poison of asps*), overindulgent (*without restraint, controlled by their every whim and passion*), savage (*and untamable*), despisers (*not a lover or friend*) of those things that are good (*hostile toward that which God has declared as very good*),

4 Betrayers that act rashly (*falling headfirst to destruction*), puffed up (*blinded by pride*), lovers of the pleasures (*of this world*) more than lovers of (*the life of*) God;

5 Having a form of godliness but denying (*Christ*) the power (*and the wisdom*) thereof: from such (*men and their teachings*) turn away.

6 For from (*men of*) this sort (*of mindset*) comes those who sneak (*stealthy*) into households, and lead (*and take*) captive idle women (*overpowering those that are weak from already being*) burdened (*and abused*) by death, led away (*into captivity, bound*) by all sorts of (*temptation to satisfy their*) lust (*for life through worldly pleasures which cannot ever quench that desire*),

7 Ever learning (*and increasing in knowledge*), but never able to come to the knowledge of the truth (*that satisfies, only found in Christ*).

8 Now as Jan'nes and Jam'bres resisted Moses, so do these also resist (*Christ, who is*) the truth: men (*who apart from*

Christ are left to reason) from crooked *(carnal)* minds, *(that are)* depraved *(and perverted)* concerning the faith.

9 But they will not advance any further *(except to more ungodliness, rather the truth will prevail)*: because their folly *(and the futility of their teaching)* will be revealed *(as to what it produces)* for all men to see, just as theirs also was.

10 But you have fully known my doctrine *(of Christ crucified, by whom the world is crucified to me, and I unto the world)*, and also my manner of life, purpose, faith, patience, love, endurance,

11 The persecutions, afflictions, which came to me at An'ti-och, at I-co'ni-um, at Lys'tra; what great persecutions I endured: but the Lord delivered me out of them all.

12 Yes and all those that desire to live *(looking)* unto the *(life and)* godliness in Christ Jesus will also suffer persecution.

13 But *(know this also that apart from Christ)* evil men *(those who are pressed in by labors and annoyances that come from death)* and those that seduce others *(leading them astray)* will continue to grow worse and worse, deceiving, and being deceived.

14 But you *(only need to)* continue in the things which you have learned *(from Christ Jesus)* and have been fully persuaded of, knowing the One from whom you have learned them;

15 And how that from a child you have known the holy scriptures, which are *(set apart and)* able to make you *(perfect and)* wise unto salvation through the faith which is in Christ Jesus our Lord.

16 All scripture is *(given and)* breathed from the heart of God *(our Father, containing Christ, the word and the wisdom that was from the beginning)* and is *(therefore)* profitable for teaching *(doctrine and instruction unto His life and Godlikeness)*, for proof *(and certainty of the testimony that has been tested and tried by fire)*, for correcting *(that which has gotten crooked)*, for instruction *(training and chastisement that leads)* unto righteousness *(which is the only life the Father ever saw fitting and has promised to us His children from the*

beginning, the same life that came out of the grave immortal in Christ Jesus):

17 So that the man (*born from the Word*) of God (*in Christ*) may be perfect (*and complete just as He is perfect and complete*), (*lacking no good thing but*) thoroughly furnished with all good works (*from the Father, so that we may walk with Him in the good fruit of His life forevermore*).

Chapter 4

1 Therefore (*since we have been given such clear evidence and sure testimony*) I urge you before God and the Lord Jesus Christ, whose *word* will judge the living and the dead at His appearing and (*the establishing of*) His kingdom (*in the earth, of which there will be no end*);

2 Proclaim (*Christ crucified*) the word (*which God has spoken to us, which we know is full of power*); be ready (*to declare that word in every situation, both*) in times that seem opportune and in times that do not; reprove (*with convincing evidence*), rebuke (*correcting erroneous beliefs*), encourage (*and comfort*) with all patience and (*sound*) doctrine.

3 Because the time will come when they will not (*esteem or*) have any patience for sound doctrine; but (*will follow*) after (*and be dictated by*) their own lusts (*for the life they can gather and*) will heap to themselves teachers, (*who will tickle the ears of their carnal minds with a message of how they can work to serve themselves with blessing and life*) having itching ears;

4 And they will turn their ears away from the truth (*where even hearing they will hear and will not understand; And seeing they will see, and not recognize*) and will (*instead*) turn aside to fables.

5 But (*soberly*) examine yourself (*that you be in the faith*) in all things, (*where you are able to*) endure afflictions, do the work of an evangelist, and be (*fully persuaded and*) completely satisfied with (*all assurance that you have entirely carried out*) your ministry (*and finished your race with confidence*).

2 Timothy 4

6 Because I am already being offered (*my blood is already pouring out*) and the time of my departure is close at hand.

7 I have fought the good fight (*never turning away from the faith*), I have finished my course, I have kept the faith (*laying hold on eternal life*):

8 There is (*but one thing that remains*) a crown of righteousness awaits me, which the Lord (*Himself*), the righteous Judge, will give me on that day (*when He adorns me with His life and immortality*): and not only me but unto all those also that love (*His life and wait for the sure hope of righteousness at*) His appearing.

9 Make your best effort to come visit me shortly:

10 Because De'mas has abandoned me for the love of this present (*evil*) world, and has departed to Thes-sa-lo-ni'ca; Cres'cens to Ga-la-tia, Ti'tus unto Dal-ma'ti-a.

11 Only Luke is here with me. Take Mark and bring him with you: because he is useful to me for (*the work of*) the ministry.

12 And Tych'i-cus have I sent to Eph'e-sus.

13 Bring the travel bag that I left at Tro'as with Car'pus, with you when you come, along with the books, and especially the parchments.

14 Alexander the coppersmith showed great hostility (*toward me, intending*) to (*harm*) me: the Lord will render to him according to (*the belief in his heart and*) the deeds (*it produces*):

15 Of whom you should also be aware, because he has greatly stood against our words.

16 At my first defense no one stood with me, but all men forsook (*and deserted*) me: I pray to God that it may not be laid to their charge.

17 In spite of all that, the Lord stood with me and strengthened me; so that through me the preaching (*of the cross of Christ*) might be fully known, and that all the Gentile nations might hear (*the faith of Jesus Christ*): and I was delivered out of the mouth of the lion.

18 And (*surely*) the Lord will deliver me from every evil (*malicious*) work and will preserve my life (*unharmed*) unto His heavenly kingdom: to whom be glory forever and ever. Amen.

19 Salute Pris'ca and A'qui-la, and the household of On-e-siph'o-rus.

20 E-ras'tus remained in Corinth: but Troph'i-mus have I left at Mi-le'tum sick.

21 Do your best to come visit before winter. Eu-bu'lus greets you, and Pu'dens, and Li'nus, and Clau'd-ia, and all the brethren (*here with me*).

22 (*May*) the Lord (*Jesus Christ*) be with your spirit. (*And His*) Grace (*and strength*) remain with you (*always*). Amen.

The Epistle of Paul to the

TITUS

The Faith Translation

Chapter 1

1 Paul, who willingly belongs to God and is an apostle and follower of Jesus Christ, according to the common faith of those who are called and have acknowledged the truth, that is according to His life and Godlikeness,

2 In the (*sure*) hope of eternal life, (*the life and immortality we see in Jesus Christ*), which God, who cannot lie, (*got down on one knee and*) promised (*us*) before the world came into being;

3 But who now in the fullness of time has revealed His word (*of promise*) through (*the word made flesh in Christ Jesus*) declaring (*the faith and the hope of the gospel to all people*), which I have been entrusted and am compelled to declare according to the will of God our Savior;

4 To Ti'tus, my true son in the faith (*that is revealed in Jesus Christ*): (*His*) Grace (*which influences our heart, that it is by His strength alone that we will share in His life, where He will show us kindness for all the ages to come*) and (*which puts our flesh to rest from all our labors*) giving us the true peace, (*that can only come*) from God the Father and the Lord Jesus Christ our Savior.

5 For this reason, I had you stay behind in Crete, so that you might set in order the things that are lacking, by selecting men of good judgment (*and sound doctrine*) as elders in every city, as I directed you:

6 If you might find those who are beyond reproach (*free of accusation*), the husband of one wife, whose children are attentive to the faith not seen as riotous or disobedient.

7 Because it is fitting (*and makes the most sense*) for an overseer to be beyond reproach, as he is the guardian (*over the affairs*) of the household of God; as not to be self-willed (*but one who prefers others*), not easily angered (*but peaceful*), not inclined to (*the abuse of*) wine (*or strong drink*), not a contentious person (*but a peacemaker*), not one who is predisposed (*and overtaken*) with a greedy desire for gain (*of power or money*).

8 But one who (*being born of God and the fruit of His life*) is a lover of strangers, having generosity toward all men, a lover of

117

Titus 1

that which is good (*seeing all men as innocent*), upright, beloved, reverent toward God, gentle and pleasant;

9 Holding close to his heart the faithful (*and sure*) word (*of our Lord Jesus*) as he has been taught (*by us*), that he may be able by (*the*) sound doctrine (*found in Christ*) to both encourage and bring the truth to light, exposing the error of those who oppose the faith.

10 For there are many who are rebellious (*refusing to submit to Christ, who is the teaching and instruction of God unto life*) they speak empty and idle words (*that can never produce eternal life*) and are seducers (*who want to exert control over men to bring them into bondage*), especially those (*who have confidence in their flesh*) of the circumcision:

11 Whose (*voices*) it is incumbent upon us to silence, (*seeing as*) they have overthrown the faith of entire households, teaching things which (*appeal to men's lust for life through the strength contained in their flesh*) disgraceful things that have no bases in the truth (*in Christ*) which they should not teach as such, so that they might gather to themselves gain (*of power or money*).

12 One of the Cre'ti-ans own poets said of them, the Cre'ti-ans are perpetual liars, and like cruel animals, who are lazy and gluttonous (*more apt to want to eat than work*).

13 This reputation sure seems accurate. For that reason, correct them sharply (*with the truth*), so that they may be grounded (*in Christ, being persuaded by*) the faith;

14 Not giving consideration to Jewish fables (*that come from those false teachers*), and to commandments from men (*who have confidence in the flesh*), that turn from, and are contrary to (*the faith and disregard*) the truth.

15 To the pure (*and innocent in heart*) all things are pure (*and undefiled*): but to those (*whose hearts*) are stained with the guilt (*brought by death do judge themselves unworthy*), and are not believing (*the truth that their death has been sent away*) see nothing as pure (*and undefiled*); because (*they are defiled from within*) even in their mind and conscience.

118

16 They proclaim that they know God; but in (*establishing*) their own works they deny Him (*not walking in His good work*), being abominable (*they make their own works their god*), refusing to be persuaded of the truth (*of His good work to give them blessing and life as a gift*), and all their works (*to gather to themselves eternal life*) are (*impotent and*) completely worthless (*in their ability to do so*).

Chapter 2

1 But speak (*boldly*) to them the things which we know contain sound doctrine (*which things are only found in the faith of Christ*):

2 So that the older men might have a clear mind (*that is free from the influences in the world*) dignified (*honored and deeply respected*), self-controlled men (*whose hope and rest is in God and not themselves*), sound in the faith, and the love of God toward them so that they might run their race with patience.

3 The elder women likewise, so that their conduct would be fitting, as one who has been captivated by the life they were set apart for (*in Christ*), not (*gossiping and*) unjustly accusing others, nor being enslaved to wine, but teachers of (*those things which are*) good (*pure, perfect and lovely*) things;

4 So that they may teach the young woman that (*the way*) to be sound in their mind (*is to have a mind that is set on His life*), where they love their husbands and love their children,

5 To be sensible, pure, nurturing their household, kind, subject to (*the Lord and honoring*) their own husbands so that the word of God would not be spoken of slanderously.

6 Encourage young men (*in the faith*) also to be sound minded (*influenced by Christ and not the world*).

7 In all (*the*) things (*you speak*) present yourself as someone in whom (*Christ has established these*) good works (*so that you might walk in them*): and declare (*the sound and incorruptible*) doctrine (*only found in Christ*) of His life and immortality, speaking with all boldness and sincerity,

Titus 2

8 Sound speech, which cannot be condemned; so that the one who is opposed to you (*trying to establish his own works*) might turn away from that which only brings him shame, having no occasion to accuse you.

9 Encourage those (*who believe upon Christ*) who are under the authority of others to be trustworthy to them, and perform well in all the things (*that are asked of them*); (*being agreeable*) not hostile or always disputing with them;

10 Not holding back (*anything from them*), but (*rather*) bearing (*the fruit of Christ's life in all*) faithfulness; so that they may (*also*) be decorated with (*His life through*) the doctrine of God our Savior in all things.

11 For the grace (*and strength*) of God that brings salvation (*from death*), has appeared (*from the grave immortal in the person of Jesus Christ, the firstborn from the dead*) to all men,

12 Teaching us about (*His lovingkindness and goodness to give us His life and immortality free from our works*), so that we would turn away from (*laboring in*) ungodliness (*from the bite of the serpent*) that told us we had to produce our own good works, but when we can see His lovingkindness to freely clothe us in His life (*and immortality in our flesh*) and justify us (*from the accusation that we were orphans who needed to establish our own lives*) we turn our back on the idea that we need to bring salvation (*from death*) to ourselves, knowing that we can walk in His (*good work and rest in Him to serve us with His*) indestructible life (*even*) in this present (*corruptible*) world;

13 (*Always*) looking (*with certainty*) for that blessed hope (*we behold in the risen Christ*), and (*patiently wait for*) the glorious appearing of the great God and our Savior Jesus Christ (*and the redemption of our bodies immortal*);

14 Who gave Himself for us, so that He might rescue us from (*perishing in death*) removing all our iniquity (*which had us laboring in lawlessness, trusting in our own works to establish our life*) and purify (*our hearts back*) to Himself, His most beloved treasure, who possess a passionate desire (*for life*) to (*walk in His*) good works (*in the life that our hearts have*

always desired and which He has prepared for us before the world began).

15 These things speak (*boldly*), encouraging, and bringing correction (*to any erroneous beliefs*) knowing that the words you speak carry the full weight of Christ; Let no man examine you (*or your authority*).

Chapter 3

1 Remind them to submit to rulers and governing authorities, and to heed (*their ordinances*), taking advantage of every opportunity to do good,

2 And to speak well of all men, and not vilifying them, but be gentle and peaceful, giving all consideration to all men.

3 Because we ourselves (*before we were persuaded of the grace of God toward us*) were sometimes foolish, unbelieving, unwilling to be persuaded (*of God's love toward us*), deceived (*having gone out of the way*), serving our various worldly lusts and pleasures (*by what we could gather to ourselves by our own hands*), living a cursed life filled with labor and annoyances, hateful (*and resentful*) of that which is good and hating one another.

4 But after the (*everlasting*) kindness and love of God our Savior was revealed toward man (*appearing in immortal flesh in the resurrection of Jesus Christ*),

5 (*Which did*) not (*come*) by works of righteousness which we performed (*with our own hands*), but according to His mercy (*and lovingkindness towards us*), He saved us (*from death*), by the washing (*away of death and corruption*) in the regeneration of man, (*physically recreating man immortal in the body of Jesus Christ, the firstborn from the dead*), and renewing (*again the promise*) of the Holy Ghost (*the Spirit of life*);

6 Which He (*has*) poured out on us abundantly through Jesus Christ our Savior;

7 That being justified by His grace (*from the accusation that we were not the sons of God*), we should be made (*heirs of God*

and) co-heirs according to the (*sure*) hope (*of the promise*) of eternal life (*the same life we see in Christ Jesus our Lord*).

8 This is the most trustworthy saying (*because God who has promised it, has also brought it to completion*), and these (*are the*) things I would like you to confidently affirm and proclaim (*both to each other and publicly*), so that they which have believed in (*the word that*) God (*has spoken in Christ to all people*) might give heed to (*this word, allowing it to give birth in their heart*) and walk in (*His*) good works (*enjoying His life*). These saying are the things which are good and profitable to all men.

9 But avoid foolish (*and worthless*) debates, and (*endless*) genealogies (*claiming special pedigree*), and arguments (*over words*), and quarreling about (*the need to perform ceremonial rituals of*) the law; for they are unprofitable and worthless (*in their ability to edify*).

10 A man that is (*still*) causing division after the first and second warning, turn away from (*and let him go, give him over to his own persuasion*);

11 Knowing that he that is doing these things has turned away from the truth (*turning it inside out*) and continues to walk out of the way that leads to life and peace, (*in the way that*) where he will condemn himself (*in his own heart*).

12 When I send Ar'te-mas to you, or Tych'i-cus, be certain to come to me in Ni-cop'o-lis: for I have determined to stay the winter there.

13 Bring Ze'nas the lawyer (*who is more of an expert in the law than a normal scribe*) and A-pol'los, well supplied with everything they need for their journey, so that they are not in want of anything.

14 And let our (*brethren*) also learn (*from the word of life you speak at Crete*) to give strict attention to establish themselves in the truth (*revealed in Christ, which will serve them*) with all that is necessary for life and Godlikeness, so that (*being persuaded to rest in His good works*) they would not be unfruitful.

15 All that are with me salute you. Greet those who love us in (*the fellowship of*) the faith (*of Jesus Christ*). Grace be with you all. Amen.

The Epistle of Paul to the

PHILEMON

The Faith Translation

Chapter 1

1 Paul, a prisoner (*for declaring the truth*) of Jesus Christ (*which truth has captivated my heart*), and Timothy our brother, to Philemon our dearly beloved, and fellow worker (*in the gospel along*) with us,

2 And to our beloved Apph'i-a, and Ar-chip'pus our fellow helper, and to the church family that meets in your house:

3 Grace to you, and peace, from God our Father and the Lord Jesus Christ.

4 I thank my God, making mention of you always in my prayers,

5 Hearing of your love and the faith that you have in the Lord Jesus, and your love for all the saints (*set part unto His life*);

6 I pray that in the fellowshipping of your faith that you may effectively communicate the knowledge of every good thing which is in you by Christ Jesus.

7 For we have great joy and are encouraged upon hearing of your love, and how because of it, the hearts of the saints are set at rest by you, brother.

8 Therefore, although I could be very bold in Christ and order you to do what seems fitting,

9 Yet for love's sake I would rather appeal to you, seeing I am now known as Paul the aged (*old man*), and also a prisoner (*for declaring the truth*) of Jesus Christ.

10 I implore you on behalf of my son (*in Christ*) O'nes'i-mus, whom I have fathered in the truth during my imprisonment:

11 Who in the past, I know was detrimental to your ministry, but he is now indeed useful to you and to me:

12 Who I have sent again to you: hoping that you would therefore receive him, that is at least, what is in my heart:

13 Who I was also hoping I could have kept with me, so that in your place he might have ministered to me in the captivity into which the preaching of the gospel has thrown me.

14 But apart from your consent I would do nothing; so that any good you might do would be born from your earnest desire and not out of any obligation.

Philemon 1

15 For perhaps he departed your life for a season, that you should now receive him forever;

16 But now not as a servant, but something greater than a servant, a beloved brother in Christ, especially beloved to me, having fathered him in the truth, but how much more to you, who is both a brother in the flesh, and in the Lord?

17 If you consider me therefore a partner with you in the gospel (*and one who also fathered you in the truth*), receive him as you would me.

18 If he has wronged you, or owes you anything, set that to my account;

19 I Paul have written this with my own hand, that I will repay it: although (*let me be clear*) I do not say that you need repay me anything even for your own self.

20 Yes, brother, let me simply have joy of you in the Lord: That reward alone is enough and refreshes my heart in the Lord.

21 Having been persuaded of the love I see has captivated and constrains your heart also, I wrote to you, knowing that (*because of your heart in Christ*) you will (*like our Lord*) also do more than I ask (*not from obligation but a willing heart born from the love of God*)

22 But would also prepare for me a lodging: because I trust that through your prayers I will be (*released and*) given to you.

23 We salute you Ep'a-phras, my fellow prisoner in Christ Jesus;

24 Mar'cus, Ar-is-tar'chus, De'mas, Lu'cas, my fellow workers.

25 The grace of our Lord Jesus Christ be with your spirit (*ever influencing your hearts and mind of His love*). Amen.

The General Epistle to the

HEBREWS

The Faith Translation

Chapter 1

1 God, who in various portions and in a multitude of ways spoke (*through and about the coming of Christ*) in former times (*when death reigned over all*) to the fathers through the prophets,

2 Has (*now*) in these last days (*before death is completely removed from the earth*) spoken to us by His Son (*Christ Jesus*), whom He has appointed the heir of all things, by whom also He created all things (*that were created*);

3 Who is (*who was, and will forever shine in*) the brightness of His glory, and the exact (*image and*) expression of His substance, (*the assurance of His person*) and (*who*) upholding all things through the (*immutable*) word of His power, when He had by (*providing*) Himself (*the lamb*) purged our death (*in His flesh*), sat down on the right hand of the Majesty on high;

4 (*Having*) been made (*a man in glorified flesh and bone forever seated in the immortality of God*), (*that which is*) far superior to the angels, as He has by (*the*) inheritance (*of God*) obtained a more excellent name than they.

5 For to which of the angels has He said at any time, "You are My Son, this day have I begotten you (*declaring you to be My Son with power in the resurrection from the dead immortal*)? And again (*with the same glory we had before the world began*), I will be to Him a Father, and he will be to me a Son?

6 And again, when He brings in the first begotten (*of many brethren*) into the world, He said, and let all the angels of God be in subjection to Him.

7 And about the angels He said, Who makes His angels like the wind and (*has created them*) His servants (*like*) a flame of fire.

8 However, to the Son He said, "Your throne, O God, is forever and ever (*without end*): the testimony of Your life (*and bodily immortality*) is (*forever*) the mark of Your kingdom."

9 You have loved the life that God can serve you with and hated (*the*) lawlessness (*of serving yourself*); therefore God,

even Your God (*and Father*) has anointed You with the oil (*of the Spirit*) of gladness above all your equals.

10 And, You Lord, in the beginning have laid the foundation of the earth; and the heavens are the works of Your hands:

11 They will (*both*) perish; but you (*will*) remain; they will all grow old like a garment does;

12 And as an old piece of clothing you will fold them up, and they will be changed (*corruptible to incorruptible*) but You are the same and Your years will not (*ever*) fail.

13 But to which of the angels said He at any time, sit on my right hand, until I make your enemies your footstool?

14 (*Not one! But*) are they not all ministering spirits, sent (*for the specific purpose*) to serve to those who will inherit the life (*and immortality*) of God?

Chapter 2

1 Therefore we ought to give more diligence to (*closely examine*) the things we have heard (*in the Son, Christ Jesus*), (*so that we do*) not ever drift away (*from the truth*).

2 Because if the word spoken (*by God and delivered*) through the angels was sure (*and unalterable*) and every overstep and refusal to listen (*to its judgment*) received (*that words*) just repayment of reward (*according to the judgment*);

3 How will we escape (*the reward*) if we neglect (*or completely disregard*) so great a salvation (*in the word spoken in the Son wherein He delivered us from death*); which (*salvation*) was first spoken by the Lord (*Jesus*) and was confirmed to us by them that heard Him;

4 (*And*) God (*Himself*) has also bore witness (*to Him*), both with signs and wonders, and with various miracles, and gifts from the Holy Ghost, (*confirming the word which is*) according to His own will (*to freely give us His life and immortality inside of flesh that can never die again*)?

5 For He has not placed the world to come in subjection to (*any of*) the angels, (*this world*) of which we are speaking.

Hebrews 2

6 But one in a certain place gave testimony, saying, what is (*it about*) man, that You are (*always*) mindful (*of and remembering Your promise*) to him? or the son of man, that You visited (*and cared for*) Him (*preserving His life from death immortal*)?

7 You made Him a little lower than the angels (*for a short while*); (*but*) You have crowned Him with glory and honor, and have set Him over (*the world to come and all*) the works of Your hands:

8 You have put all things (*in heaven and earth*) in subjection under His feet. And in that He put all in subjection under Him, He left out nothing that is not put under Him. But now we do not yet see all things put under Him.

9 But we see Jesus, who was made a little lower than the angels because of the suffering of death (*in the flesh*), (*who has been*) decorated with (*the*) glory (*of God inside of flesh that will never die again*) and in honor (*seated at the Father's right hand*); so that He through the grace (*and everlasting kindness*) of God should taste death for every man.

10 For it is only fitting for Him, for whom all things (*were made*) and by whom all things (*were made*), in bringing many sons to (*the same*) glory (*and immortality*), to make the author of their salvation perfect (*by raising Him up a new man free from death in the image and likeness of God*) through suffering (*of death in the flesh*).

11 Because both He that cleanses (*them*) from death, and they who are cleansed from death (*and have been set apart for His life*) are all one (*flesh*): for that reason, He is not ashamed to call them (*His*) brothers.

12 Saying, I will declare Your name (*Father*) to My brothers in the middle of the assembly (*of those You have set apart for Your life*) will I sing praises to You (*crying out unto You who is able to save Me from death*).

13 And again (*He declared in another place*); I will put My trust in Him (*to rescue Me from death*). And again (*saying*), behold (*both*) I and the children which God has given Me (*will be saved*).

14 Since therefore the children had partaken of flesh and (*were corrupted by*) blood He also Himself likewise (*willingly*) took part in the same (*death that this served them*), so that by His death He might destroy the one who held the dominion of death, (*that slanderous accuser*) the devil;

15 And (*so that He could*) deliver (*setting free*) those who through the fear of death were all their lifetime were held (*captive*) in bondage.

16 For surely, He did not take on (*the appearance of*) angels; but took the place of (*a man born*) the seed of Abraham.

17 Therefore in all things it was fitting for Him to come in the likeness of His brothers, so that He might become a merciful and trustworthy high priest (*of men*) in all things pertaining to God, to show Himself gracious in removing (*the suffering at the hands of*) death from the people.

18 For given that He Himself has (*also*) suffered being tempted (*by death to preserve His own life as they are*), He is able to powerfully rescue them that are tempted (*removing their fear of death*).

Chapter 3

1 Therefore (*we, His*) brothers who have been set apart for the same life, (*made to be*) partakers of the heavenly calling, (*should*) carefully consider Christ Jesus, the apostle and high priest of the faith we profess (*for He is God's message to us; God Himself, ministering life to us*);

2 Who was faithful (*being the full expression of the faith*) from Him that appointed Him (*the High Priest over His entire house*), as also Moses was faithful in all His house.

3 But this man (*Christ Jesus*) was considered fitting of greater honor than Moses, because (*He built the house and*) He who has built the house has more honor than the house.

4 For every house is built by some man (*both those of greater and lesser honor*); but He that built all things is God.

5 And Moses was certainly faithful in all His house, as a servant, because (*he gave*) a testimony (*pertaining to*) those

things which were to be spoken after (*by God Himself in Christ*);

6 But Christ (*was faithful*) as the Son over His own house (*being fully persuaded of God's faithfulness towards mankind, to provide Himself the lamb to sanctify us from death and also being fully persuaded of the Father's faithfulness towards Him to raise Him from the dead*); Whose house we are, if truly our hearts are apprehended (*by Him*) being confident and rejoicing in the sure hope (*of His same life*) that endures to the end.

7 Therefore as the Holy Ghost said (*testifying about Christ*), today if you will hear His voice (*and rest in the work which God has done in Him*),

8 Harden not your hearts as (*your fathers did*) when they rebelled (*in unbelief*), in the day of temptation (*in drought*) in the wilderness:

9 When your fathers tempted Me, to prove Myself (*and My goodness toward them*) and having seen My works for forty years (*still would not rest in My goodness and strength to give them the promised land as their inheritance*).

10 Therefore was I grieved with that generation, and said, they do always go astray in their heart, and they have not known My ways (*because death has put a veil over their hearts*).

11 So (*being grieved*) I swore in My wrath (*to destroy death knowing*) that they could not (*ever*) enter My rest (*by the works of their own hands*).

12 Listen diligently, (*therefore*) brothers (*to hear the word which God has spoken in Christ*), so that (*after beholding the work that God has done to conquer death and raise you to His life*) there would not remain in any of you an evil heart (*which is one filled with the work you must do to rescue yourself from destruction, which comes*) from unbelief, in departing from (*trusting in*) the living God (*the only immortal, to serve you with His life*).

13 But encourage (*yourselves and*) each other daily (*fellowshipping around the work that God has done in Christ*), while it is called today; so that none of you would have a heart

hardened through the deceitfulness (*that comes*) from death (*not partaking of and resting in His good work*).

14 Because we are made partakers (*of the life*) of Christ, if indeed we (*are fully persuaded of the work that God did*) being apprehended by (*the faith of Jesus Christ*) the beginning (*and end*) of our assurance (*of His same life*), (*the hope which*) endures to the end;

15 As it is said, today if you will hear His voice, harden not your hearts, as in (*the day of*) the rebellion (*in the wilderness*).

16 Because some, when they had heard (*His voice and saw His works forty years*), did rebel (*in unbelief*): however not all that came out of Egypt by Moses (*rebelled*).

17 But who was it that grieved Him forty years? was it not those who (*after seeing all His mighty works for forty years continued*) in unbelief, trusting in the strength of their own hands to preserve their lives (*from destruction*) whose bodies fell (*dead*) in the wilderness?

18 And to whom He did swear (*in His passion for the life that only He could serve them with, being grieved*) that they could not enter into His rest (*through the strength of their own hands*), but unto those who disobeyed (*not resting in His good work*)?

19 So we see that they could not enter in because (*their heart*) of unbelief (*because their hearts being consumed with the works of their own hand, could never allow them to rest in His work*).

Chapter 4

1 Let us therefore hearken diligently (*to hear His voice*) with all reverence (*and harden not our hearts*) so that we (*also*) do not forsake (*or depart from*) the promise of entering into His rest, lest anyone think they come short of the promise (*of His life and immortality*).

2 For unto us was the good news preached as well as unto them (*that it is through God and His strength alone that we will enter into His promised rest*): but the word they heard had no

benefit to them, not being joined together (*united*) with the faith in them that heard it (*and refused to rest in the promise even after seeing His works for forty years*).

3 Because we which have believed (*on the good work that God has done in Christ*) do enter into (*His*) rest (*and have ceased from our own works*), as He said, As I have sworn in My passion (*for the incorruptible life which only I can serve them with*), being grieved, because they cannot enter into My rest (*having sought it by their own works*): although the works (*which I have done for them to enter into*) were finished from the foundation of the world (*before death entered*).

4 Because He spoke in this certain place about the seventh day, when it says; And God rested the seventh day from all His works (*which works He prepared for us to walk therein*).

5 And (*He says*) again in this place (*in the wilderness*) that they did not enter into My rest.

6 Therefore (*we see that*) there remains a rest for some to enter into (*that causes them to cease from their own works*), and they to whom the good news was first preached did not enter in because of their disobedience to the faith (*who after seeing the work of God, refused to rest therein but continued to trust in their own works and perished in the wilderness*):

7 And again, He speaks about another day, through David saying, today, after so long a time, as it is said; today if you will hear His voice, harden not your hearts.

8 Because if Joshua had given them rest (*where they ceased from their own works*), then He would not afterward have spoken of another day.

9 There remains therefore a (*Sabbath*) rest (*revealed in the faith of Jesus Christ*) for the people of God (*where they rest in His life and immortality and do no work, and He will be their God and they will be His people*).

10 For he that has entered into that rest (*which Christ' death and resurrection brings*), has also ceased from his own works, as God did from His.

11 Therefore we should be diligent (*to hearken unto the faith of Jesus Christ*) to enter into His rest, so that no one would fall

(*into the condemnation that death serves*) after the same example of disobedience (*in those who fell in the wilderness refusing God's work for their own*).

12 Because the word which God has spoken in (*the faith of*) Jesus Christ is alive (*energized*) and full of power, and is sharper than any two-edged sword, able to penetrate through both the soul and the spirit from the joints and marrow (*of a man's heart*) and is the discerner of all the thoughts and intentions of the heart.

13 And there is not any creature hidden from before His eyes. But rather all things are uncovered and laid bare to Him who has (*given*) His word and testimony (*about us*).

14 Seeing then that we have a great high priest, who is passed into the heavens (*in glorified human flesh, forever free from death*), Jesus the Son of God, let us continue to hold firm (*to keep hearing the faith, so that*) the confession (*of our hearts be united together with His*).

15 For we do not have a high priest who cannot sympathize with the feeling of our death; but He was in all points tempted (*by death*) the same way we are, yet without ever enlisting His own ability to save Himself (*but cried out to the One who could save Him from death*).

16 We should come therefore with boldness (*and frankness of speech*) to the throne of (*His*) grace (*and strength to overcome death*), so that we may (*also*) receive mercy (*to escape the death and corruption that is in the world through lust*) and (*where we will*) find (*rest in*) His grace to strengthen us in our time of need.

Chapter 5

1 For every high priest (*since they are*) taken from among men are appointed for men in things pertaining to God, so that they may offer both gifts and sacrifices for death:

2 Who (*also being a man*) can have compassion on the ones who are ignorant, and on them that are (*willfully going*) out of

the way; because he himself is also clothed with the infirmity (*of the body of death*).

3 And for that reason, just as he is obligated (*to make an offering*) for the people, so also (*must he make offering*) for himself, for death.

4 And no man receives this honor from himself, but he must be called of God, as was Aaron.

5 So also Christ did not glorify Himself to be made a high priest; but He that said unto Him, "You are My Son, today have I begotten you", (*He has appointed Him*).

6 As He said also in another place, "You are a priest (*to the world*) forever (*without beginning or end*) after the image of Melchisedec.

7 Who in the days of His (*suffering of affliction in the*) flesh, when He had offered up (*His own body with*) prayers and strong crying and tears from a meek and lowly heart unto the (*only*) One that was able to save Him from death and was heard in that He (*was fully persuaded that He*) revered God's strength alone (*to deliver Him from death*);

8 Though He was a Son, yet He learned by harkening diligently (*to the word of promise from the Father to save Him*) from the things which He suffered (*in the flesh*);

9 And having been made perfect (*raised unto the likeness of God in glorified human flesh*) He became the author of eternal salvation unto all of those who harken diligently to (*hear*) Him;

10 Called (*and appointed*) of God, a high priest after the image of Melchisedec (*who sits forever in the power of an endless life in immortal flesh*).

11 Concerning whom we have many things to say (*to you*), which are hard to be understood and difficult to be interpreted, seeing as you are slothful (*not being diligent*) in your hearing.

12 For by this time when you ought to be teachers, you (*still*) need someone to teach you again the beginning teachings of the utterances of God (*contained in the law which were always pointing to Christ*); and have become like babes that still have need of milk and cannot handle strong meat.

13 Because everyone that (*has been slothful in their hearing*) needs milk and are without experience or understanding (*still being ignorant*) of the word (*contained in the law that spoke*) of God's righteousness towards us to (*provide Himself the lamb that would cleanse us from death once and forever and*) serve us with His life and immortality (*as our inheritance*): for he is a babe.

14 But strong meat belongs to those who are of full age (*mature*), the ones who have had their senses exercised (*after having grappled with an unconcealed heart are persuaded by the word contained in the law of God's righteousness toward them and who now look to the faith of Jesus Christ and are able*) to discern between that which is born from the word of life and that which brings death.

Chapter 6

1 Therefore leaving behind the beginning teachings of Christ (*that came through the gifts and sacrifices of the law*), let us move on to perfection (*where we rest looking to the faith of Jesus Christ wherein we were once and for all time sanctified from death by the blood of Christ, the lamb of God and not by washings, cleansings and sacrifices from the blood of bulls and goats which could never make us perfect unto immortality in our flesh*), not laying again the foundation of these offerings which (*were only a shadow to keep us and teach us until Christ, the substance, would come but which*) had no power to purge our conscience from (*death and from performing those*) dead works and renew a heart filled with faith toward God (*where we rested from our own works*),

2 (*Moving on*) from the (*beginning*) teachings (*and rituals*) of washings (*that could not ever cleanse us from our dying flesh*) and the laying on of hands, and the of resurrection of the dead and of eternal judgment (*which things were only ever a shadow, but the substance was always pointing to the faith that would come in Christ*).

Hebrews 6

3 And these sacrifices and offerings we will move on from, God willing (*once we see what the law was truly speaking about and go to rest in Christ sacrifice that sanctified us from death once and for all time*).

4 Because it is impossible for those who (*have seen the word that the law was always speaking about was Christ, who has forever sanctified us from death*) having been once enlightened (*by that teaching in the law*), and have tasted of the gift of God from heaven, and saw they were offered the same share in the gift of the Holy Spirit (*and the life which He brings*);

5 And have tasted the goodness of the word of God (*in Christ*), and the strength (*and glorification*) of the world to come (*if they reject His sacrifice; for them to find their heart renewed and filled with faith toward God*),

6 If they (*who were once enlightened, reject His sacrifice and*) turn aside (*from Christ but continue performing the dead works contained in ceremonies and sacrifices of the law*), (*it is impossible for them to find that those sacrifices are able*) to renew their conscience (*where they rest and do no work*); seeing as they crucify to themselves continually the Son of God (*considering the blood He shed as common as the blood of bulls and goats, where they disesteem*) putting Him (*and the word which He has spoken*) to public shame (*and never finding their conscience renewed where they rest from their own works with their faith toward God*).

7 For (*just as*) the earth which drinks in the rain that often comes on it brings forth fruit fitting for them for whose sake it was made and by whom it was also tilled, (*so also do we*) receive the fruit of God's life (*when we are diligent with His word, to hear and soak in that which has rained from heaven in Christ, settling it in our heart*):

8 But (*just as*) the land that (*does not receive the rain*) produces thorns and briers is rejected (*and barren to them*) and is near to (*being under*) a curse, and that land's end is only to be burned up (*and consumed in the fire, so are the dead works of those who refuse to rest in His good work*).

9 However, beloved we are persuaded of better things about you, and of all the things that accompany the salvation (*wherein He has rescued our lives from death and corruption, serving us with all the fruit of His life unto immortality in our flesh*), even though we have spoken (*frankly*) in this manner.

10 Because God is not unjust to forget the works of you (*that were born*) from (*His*) love (*toward you*), which (*work*) you have shown toward His name (*being diligent to hear Him*), whereby you have (*continually*) ministered (*His love*) to the saints and do (*still*) minister.

11 And we desire that every one of you do show the same diligence to (*hear the faith that keeps you in*) the full assurance of hope (*of His same life being formed in you*) which endures to the end:

12 That you would be not slothful (*hearers*), but followers of them who through (*the hearing of the faith*) are fully persuaded, and (*being certain*) do patiently wait for (*resting in*) the promise of His life and immortality.

13 For when God made promise to Abraham (*that he would be the father of many nations*), because He could swear by no one greater, He swore by Himself,

14 Saying, surely blessing I will bless you (*with many descendants*) and multiplying I will multiply you (*and your descendants like the stars in the sky and the sand on the seashore*).

15 And so, after he had patiently waited (*believing upon the One who had spoken to him*), he obtained the promise.

16 For men do (*always*) swear by the greater: and take an oath that establishes a guarantee (*that creates confidence*) to them and brings an end to all (*arguments and*) contradictions.

17 Wherein God, desiring more abundantly to show the heirs of the promise the (*unalterable and*) unchangeableness of His purpose (*and will*), confirmed it by (*swearing by Himself*) an oath:

18 That by two unchangeable things, in which it was impossible for God to lie, (*so that in this*) we might have strong comfort (*and confidence*), (*we*) who have (*all our days*) fled

(*looking*) for refuge (*and help*) to lay hold upon the (*certainty of the*) hope (*that is now*) set before us:

19 Which hope we now have (*in Christ*) as an anchor of the soul, which contains both a certainty and unchangeability, and which (*gives the confidence to*) enter into (*His rest*) which is behind the veil;

20 Where the forerunner has for us (*already*) entered, even Jesus Christ, made a high priest (*to the world*) forever (*without beginning or end*) after the image of Melchisedec (*who sits forever in the power of an endless life in immortal flesh*).

Chapter 7

1 For this Melchisedec, king of Salem, priest of the most high God, who met Abraham returning from the slaughter of the kings (*bringing him gifts of bread and wine*), and (*who*) blessed him (*saying, blessed are you from the most high God, the possessor of heaven and earth*);

2 To this Melchisedec also Abraham divided a tenth part of all (*the goods*); first being interpreted King of righteousness (*possessing the life which God saw as it ought to be*), and after that also King of Salem, which is (*interpreted*), King of peace;

3 Without father, without mother, without descendants, having neither beginning of days, nor end of life; but made like unto the image of the Son of God; who abides a priest (*to the world*) continually (*in perpetuity*).

4 Now consider how great (*Abraham recognized*) this man was, that even the founding father offered the tenth of all the goods.

5 For indeed those who are from the sons of Levi have received the office of the priesthood, and have a commandment to take a tenth from the people according to the law, and that is, from their brethren, even though they have come out of the lions of Abraham:

6 But he who has no descendants (*whose ancestry*) is not counted from the sons of Levi received a tenth from Abraham and blessed him, the one who received the promise (*of His life and immortality*).

7 Apart now from any and all dispute (*we can say with certainty that*) the lesser (*possessing no ability to serve himself with life and immortality*) is blessed from the greater (*the only immortal, the possessor of heaven and earth*).

8 And here men that die receive the tenth; but there the one who received them, is one of whom it testifies that he lives (*forever without end of days*).

9 And if I may so say, Levi also, who received the tenth under the law, paid the tenth in Abraham.

10 Because he was yet in the lions of his father (*Abraham*) when Melchisedec met him.

11 Therefore if perfection (*where seeing your death has been sent away once and for all time, and you rest from all your work in the promise of His life unto immortality in your flesh*) were to come through the Levitical priesthood, (for under that priesthood the people received the law), why would there be any need for another priesthood to rise after the image of Melchisedec, and not be called after the image of Aaron's priesthood?

12 But because the priesthood (*of Aaron was inferior in its ability to bring perfection, it needed to be*) changed, and therefore by necessity there would also be a change of the law.

13 Because He (*who is called of God a high priest after the image of Melchisedec*) of whom these things are spoken (*and prophesied of Christ Jesus our Lord*), belongs to another tribe, from which (*tribe*) no man has served at the altar.

14 For it is apparent that our Lord Jesus has sprung from out of Judah; of which tribe Moses spoke nothing concerning the priesthood.

15 But it is even more apparent: that after the resemblance of Melchisedec there would arises another priest,

16 Who is made (*the high priest of God*), not according to (*the weakness and inferiority of*) performing the carnal commandments (*and ceremonies*) under the law, but according to the power of an endless life (*in His resurrection from the dead*).

Hebrews 7

17 Because He testified (*about Him saying*), You are a priest forever after the image of Melchisedec (*without beginning or end, in perpetuity*)

18 For there is indeed a disannulling (*a putting away of that priesthood that was*) of the commandment (*being that it was only ever a shadow of good things to come and was*) beforehand intended to be done away with because of the weakness and unprofitableness of it to bring (*perfection to the hearers*).

19 For the law (*of commandment*) made nothing perfect (*immortal*), but the bringing in of a better hope (*in bodily resurrection of Jesus Christ*) did; by (*the hearing of*) which (*faith*) we draw near to God (*unto perfection; His life unto immortality in our flesh*).

20 To the degree that He was not made a priest without an oath (*but God Himself swore an oath*):

21 Because those priests (*from Aaron's priesthood*) were made (*priests*) without an oath; but this (*man*) with an oath by the One that said unto Him, The Lord (*Himself*) has sworn and will not repent, you are a priest forever after the image of Melchisedec:

22 By so much (*more then*) was Jesus made (*a high priest that is*) the certainty of a better covenant (*which is able to bring us to perfection; in the same life and immortality that is in Him*).

23 And truly (*under this old priesthood*) there were many priests that were not allowed to continue by reason of death:

24 But this man, because He lives forevermore (*in glorified flesh that can never die again*) He has an unchangeable priesthood.

25 Therefore He is able also to save them to the uttermost (*completely healing them from the sting of death unto immortality in their flesh*) who come to God through Him, seeing as He ever lives to make intercession in their hearts (*of the certainty of His same life manifested in them*).

26 For truly it was fitting for us (*and for the life God promised us from the beginning*) to have a high priest who is holy, (*set

apart for the life that cannot ever die), innocent (of death's accusation), undefiled (by death), (forever) separated from death and who was made (in immortal flesh so that He could ascend in it) higher than the heavens;

27 Who does not need to daily, as those (Levitical) high priests to offer up sacrifice, first for His own death, and then for the people's (death): because this He did one time (sanctifying all from death) when He offered up Himself.

28 Because the law makes men high priests who have (the) infirmity (of death in their flesh); but the word of the oath (which He swore declares the Son a high priest after the power of an endless life), which changes the law, making the Son (a high priest), who is perfected (in an immortal human body at the right hand of the Father) forevermore.

Chapter 8

1 Now of all the things which we have spoken (to you) this is the principal thing: We now have a high priest such as this, who sat down on the right hand of the throne of the Majesty in the heavens (a man in glorified flesh and bone that cannot ever die again);

2 A minister (who serves continually) in the holy of holies (having already entered into the place set apart and prepared for you), and from the true tabernacle (of God) which the Lord has built and fastened together, and not man's hands.

3 Because every high priest is appointed so that they can offer gifts and sacrifices (for the people): for which reason it is necessary that this man also would have something to offer (which was His own blood).

4 Because if He were on the earth, He would not be a priest (of the heavenly), seeing as the (earthly) priests that offer gifts (and sacrifices by the sprinkling the blood of bulls and goats to the purification of the flesh do so only as an example) according to (the pattern given in) the law:

5 Which serve (only) as the example and shadow of heavenly things (and not the very substance), as Moses was admonished

143

of God when he was about to make the tabernacle: for, See, He said, that you make all things according to the pattern which I showed to you on the mountain.

6 But now has He (*as our high priest*) obtained a more excellent ministry (*who after being sanctified from death once and for all time, appeared in the heavenly tabernacle in immortal flesh and bone with His own blood*), by how much greater (*of a ministry*) is He now also the arbitrator of a better testament, which was established upon better promises (*of the same life and immortality in our flesh*).

7 For if that first (*priesthood of the old*) covenant (*along with its sacrifices in the earthly tabernacle made after the pattern given in the law*) had been free from fault (*able to bring perfection, purging a man's conscience from death where they rested in the work that God has done to perfect them once and for all time unto immortality in their flesh*) there would have been no desire for the second.

8 Therefore finding fault with those things (*which were only ever meant to serve as a shadow pointing to the very substance*), He said, Behold, the days are coming, says the Lord, when I will make a new covenant with the house of Israel and with the house of Judah:

9 Not according to the covenant (*that only testified of the promise good things to come but was not the substance*) that I made with their fathers in the day when I took them by the hand to lead them out (*of the bondage*) of the land of Egypt; because (*in that covenant*) they (*did not rest in the works of My hand but*) continued (*to trust in the works of their own hands and*) not in My covenant (*although I was a husband to them*), and I disregarded their works (*which only served them with the fruit of death and could never allow them to rest in Me to care for them and serve them with My life and immortality*), saith the Lord.

10 But this is the covenant that I will make with the house of Israel after those days, says the Lord; I will put My (*Spirit into them and My*) teaching and instruction into their minds and write it on their hearts (*the work which I have done to provide*

144

Myself the lamb to remove their death once and for all time): *(so that)* I will be to them a God, and they will be to Me a people *(where they reap all the fruit of My life where they have not sown)*:

11 And they will not need to teach every man his neighbor, and every man teach his brother, saying, know the Lord: because *(I will place My Spirit within them)* all will know Me *(intimately as Father)*, from the least to the greatest.

12 Because I will be merciful to *(remove from them)* the injustice death has brought them and their death and *(the sting of)* iniquity, *(along with all the fruit of death that it served them)* will I remember no more.

13 In that He said, A new covenant, He has immediately made the first one obsolete *(declaring that it was decaying and growing old and that it would pass away because it was not sufficient for them to rest in Him to be their God and they to be His people)*. Now that which decays and that which grows old is already near to vanish away.

Chapter 9

1 Now certainly the first *(covenant pointed to the promise and)* also had *(high priests performing)* acts of service *(for the people as established by the law, which service was a shadow testifying about how God would purge them from death)* and *(also had)* the earthly sanctuary *(that was made after the pattern which God showed Moses)*.

2 For there was a tabernacle prepared; the first room *(that the priests would enter every sabbath)*, containing the candlestick, and the table and the shewbread; which is called the Holy place.

3 Now behind the second veil was the *(second)* tabernacle which is called the Holiest of all;

4 Which *(the high priest must enter every year with blood, having)* the golden censer *(to carry burning coals from the altar of incense to behind the veil)*, and the ark of the covenant covered all around with gold, wherein was the golden pot that

had manna, and Aaron's rod that budded, and the tablets of testimony;

5 And over the ark the cherubims of glory shadowing the mercy seat; concerning which it is not now the time to speak in detail.

6 Now (*for that present time*) when these things were thus ordained (*and in place*), the priests always went (*every sabbath*) into (*the Holy place*) the first tabernacle, accomplishing the service (*for the people*) of God.

7 But into the second (*tabernacle behind the veil*) the high priest went in alone and only once every year, and not without blood, which he offered for himself, and for the errors of the people (*who had ignorantly gone out of the way unto life*):

8 The Holy Ghost was signifying (*by this*), that the way into the Holiest of all (*in the true heavenly tabernacle*) was not yet made manifest, while as the earthly tabernacle (*along with its gifts and sacrifices*) were still in place:

9 Which was only a shadow for that specific period of time, in which both gifts and sacrifices were offered, that could not ever make the one that did the service perfect, as pertaining to (*purging of the*) conscience (*from the death in their flesh*);

10 But only consisted in meats and drinks, and divers' washings, and carnal ordinances, imposed on them (*to keep them shut up unto the faith*) until the time of reformation (*when God would make straight that which got crooked purging our conscience of our body of death*).

11 However, Christ having appeared (*in the holiest place*), coming as a high priest (*the substance*) of the good things to come, (*who came*) by a greater and more perfect tabernacle (*in the heavens*), not made with hands, that is to say, not of this (*earthly*) building (*of which we have spoken*);

12 Neither (*has He entered*) by the blood of goats and calves, but by His own blood He entered in once into the true Holiest of all (*in the heavens*), having (*once and forever*) obtained eternal redemption (*from death*) for us all.

13 For if the (*continued offering of the*) blood of bulls and goats, and the burnt ashes of a heifer (*mixed with water and*)

sprinkled upon those spotted by death, (*was meant to keep us*), sanctifying (*our hearts by pointing us*) to the purifying of the flesh (*which was to come*):

14 How much more will the blood of Christ, who through the eternal Spirit offered Himself (*once and for all time and appeared with His own blood, His flesh clothed with immortality, forever*) unspotted (*by death*) to God, purge your conscience from performing dead works to serve the living God?

15 And because of this, He is the mediator (*the One who guarantees all the terms*) of a new (*and better*) covenant, so that by means of (*His*) death, for the redemption of the transgressions (*deviations, and willful disregard*) there was under the first covenant, (*so that being released from the bondage of death*) all those who are called (*His son's*) might receive the promise of eternal inheritance.

16 Because where there is a will, there must also of necessity be the death of the one who made it.

17 For a will is only in force after men are dead: otherwise, it is of no strength at all while the one who has made it lives.

18 For that same reason neither was the first (*covenant*) set apart as sanctified without (*the shedding of*) blood.

19 For when Moses had spoken every precept to (*instruct*) all the people according to the law, he took the blood of calves and of goats, mixed with water, and scarlet wool, and hyssop, and sprinkled both the book (*of the covenant*), and all the people,

20 Saying, this is the blood that testifies of all that God (*will do which He*) has charged (*be done*) concerning you.

21 Then he sprinkled with blood both the tabernacle, and all the vessels of the ministry.

22 And almost all (*the patterns of heavenly*) things are by the law purged with blood (*in the earthly tabernacle*); because apart from the shedding of blood there is no sending away (*of death*).

23 It was therefore necessary that the patterns of things (*which were only representative of things*) in the

heavens, should be purified with these (*sacrifices*); but the heavenly things themselves with better sacrifices than these (*which by the law were only patterns*).

24 For Christ has not entered into the holy places made with hands, which are the figures of the true; but (*has entered*) into heaven itself, now to appear in the presence of God for us:

25 Nor (*has He entered*) that He should offer Himself often (*annually*), as the high priest enters into the holiest place every year with blood of another (*kind and not their own*);

26 Otherwise, it would have been necessary for Him to have offered Himself repeatedly (*for our death*) since the foundation of the world (*when death first entered*), but now once near the culmination of the age (*of death's reign*) has He appeared to put away death (*once and for all time*) through the sacrifice of Himself.

27 And in the same way it is appointed unto men once to die, but after this the judgment:

28 So Christ was also offered once to bear the transgressions which brought death to many (*sending their death away*); and unto them that patiently wait for Him will He appear the second time (*from heaven*) apart from death (*bringing justice*) unto the salvation (*of our bodies immortal subduing the earth cleansing it of every remnant of death, joining heaven and earth as one*).

Chapter 10

1 For the law having a shadow of good things to come (*through the faith revealed in Jesus Christ*), but not the very shape and substance of the things, can never with those sacrifices (*of bulls and goats*) which they offered year by year continually make those who (*desire to*) draw near to (*God*) perfect (*in their conscience, where they come boldly with full assurance to Him for reward having been once and for all time purged from death to serve the living God*).

2 Otherwise would they not have ceased to be offered? because the worshippers (*seeing they were*) once purged (*from*

death) should no longer have a conscience that is (*filled with laboring and toiling to preserve their own lives*) from death.

3 But in those sacrifices, there is a remembrance made again every year of (*the*) death (*that looms over them*).

4 Because it is not possible that the blood of bulls and of goats could ever send away (*conquering the*) death (*in a man's flesh*).

5 For that reason when He came into the world (*as a man*), He said, (*Abba, You have opened My ears*) sacrifice and offering (*of the blood of bulls and goats*) You did not desire (*from Me*). however, a body have You prepared Me (*that I might provide Myself the lamb*)

6 In burnt offering and sacrifice (*of bulls and goats*) for (*their*) death You have had no pleasure (*because those offerings could never satisfy Your desire to be with them and stand face to face with them in Your love, forever*).

7 Then I said, behold (*I AM*), in the volume (*and the midst of the scroll*) of the book it is written of Me. (*I AM manifest in the flesh*) to fulfill Your will O God (*to provide Myself, the lamb*).

8 After when He said, Sacrifice and offering and burnt offerings (*of the blood of bulls and goats*) for (*their*) death You did not desire of Me, neither did You have pleasure (*where Your will was forever satisfied*) in those (*sacrifices*); which are offered according to the law;

9 Then said He, behold, I delight to do Your will, O God. (*In which*) He abolishes (*the necessity for*) the first (*sacrifices contained in the law which were only ever a shadow*), that He may establish the second (*which is able to bring about His will and satisfy His desire to be with man forever*).

10 By which will we are sanctified (*from death*) through the offering of the body of Jesus Christ once and for all time.

11 But yet every priest stands serving daily (*at the altar*) and offering repeatedly the same sacrifices, which cannot ever send away death:

12 But this man, after He had offered Himself one time as the sacrifice for (*our*) death forever, sat down on the right hand of God;

Hebrews 10

13 From then on expectantly waiting (*for the sure hope*) until (*the day*) His enemies (*death and the grave*) are made His footstool (*in all the earth*).

14 Because by the one offering (*of Himself*) has He perfected forever those that are purified (*from death having been set apart for His life*).

15 Whereof the Holy Ghost also is a witness to us: because after that He has said,

16 This is the covenant that I will make with them after those days, says the Lord; I will put My (*Spirit into them and My*) teaching and instruction into their minds and write it on their hearts (*the work which I have done to provide Myself the lamb to remove their death once and for all time*);

17 And their death and (*the sting of*) iniquity, (*along with all the fruit of death that it served them*) will I remember no more.

18 Now where death is sent away there is no longer an offering for iniquity (*because the ones who see they were once and for all time purged from death rest from their labor to preserve their own lives*).

19 Having therefore, brothers, boldness to enter (*with confidence*) into the holiest place (*where we with an unveiled face may stand face to face with God*) by the blood of (*the Lamb*) Jesus,

20 By a new and living way, which He has authored (*and set apart*) for us through the veil, that is to say, through His flesh (*being rent for our body of death*);

21 And having a (*greater*) high priest (*who lives forever in glorified flesh*) over the house of God;

22 Let us then draw near (*to Him and enter*) with a genuine heart with the full assurance of the faith (*of Jesus Christ*), having our hearts sprinkled (*clean*) from a conscience filled with our own works and our flesh washed clean (*where our members go to rest*) in the pure water (*of the word of His testimony about us*).

23 Let us hold fast to the (*same*) confession of our (*sure*) hope without wavering; for the One who promised (*us the same life and immortality*) is trustworthy (*to perform it*).

24 And let us think of one another to stir up (*each another*) to love and to (*rest in His*) good works:

25 Not abandoning the gathering of ourselves together, as is common among some, but (*gathering together to*) exhort one another (*of the sure hope we have in Him*): and so much more so as we see the day (*of salvation*) approaching (*where all death and corruption in the earth will be removed in His return*).

26 Because if we willfully disregard (*rejecting His sacrifice*) and forfeit our share in His life after we have received the knowledge of the truth (*that He is the lamb God provided for our death that the law was always speaking about*), there remains no other sacrifice for death,

27 But (*only*) a certain fearful expectation of the judgment and fiery zeal (*that is coming to remove every remnant of death from the earth*), which (*fire*) will devour all the enemies (*on the last day*).

28 He that despised (*and rejected the mercy spoken of in*) Moses law died without (*receiving its*) mercy under two or three witnesses:

29 Of how much worse a punishment (*of death that came from transgressing the law*), do you think would be deemed fitting (*of comparison*), (*for the one*) who has (*treated with disregard, having*) trampled underfoot the Son of God, and has considered the blood of the testament (*which secured the promise*) by which (*blood*) he was sanctified (*from death*), an ordinary thing (*thinking of it as common as the blood of bulls and goats*), and has done despite to (*rejecting*) the Spirit of grace (*which punishment in comparison seems like no punishment at all should one perish in the second death on the last day*)?

30 For we know Him Who has promised, Vengeance belongs to Me, I will recompense (*for death and reward with My life and immortality*), says the Lord. And again, The Lord will bring His (*mercy and*) justice to His people.

31 It is a fearful thing (*for the one expecting punishment and not reward*) to fall into the hands of the living God (*that though He has mercy in His hands they flee in fear unto destruction*).

Hebrews 10

32 But rather keep in remembrance the former days, where after you were first enlightened (*by the truth revealed in the faith of Jesus Christ*), how you endured a great struggle of sufferings;

33 Whereby were you indeed made a spectacle both by reviling (*insults*) and tribulations (*and persecution*); because you became partners along with those that were so reproached.

34 Because you had compassion for me in my bonds and accepted the spoiling of your goods joyfully, knowing in your hearts that you have a better and more enduring (*incorruptible*) substance (*reserved for you*) in heaven.

35 Cast not away therefore your confidence (*in the sure hope of the same life revealed in Jesus Christ*), which has great recompence of reward.

36 For you have need of patience (*which this hope and confidence brings you*), so that after you have trusted in the will of God (*to clothe you with His life*), you might receive the promise.

37 For in yet a little while, and the One who (*has promised He*) will come, will (*of a certainty*) come, and (*though men may think it be delayed, wait for it; because it will surely come*) it will not delay.

38 Now the just (*who rest in the certainty of Him to decorate them with all the fruit of His life unto immortality in their flesh*) will live by the faith (*revealed*) of Jesus Christ: but if any man draws back (*cowering away in fear*), (*He has said*) My soul will have no pleasure in him (*who perishes running unto destruction*).

39 But we are not of them who draw back (*in fear*) unto destruction; but of them that are fully persuaded (*of the faith revealed in the death, burial, and bodily resurrection of Jesus Christ*) unto the complete wholeness of the entire person (*to appear in His same life and immortality*).

Chapter 11

1 Now (*the word that was with God, that originated from God and was God, has come and perfected His promise inside of human flesh*) the word made immortal flesh (*in the resurrection of Jesus Christ, who*) is the substance of the faith, (*the originator and the perfecter*) that gives the full assurance of everything ever hoped for, and provides the indisputable evidence, proving (*the certainty of*) that which is not yet seen.

2 For by that word (*which was from the beginning*) the elders obtained a good report (*of the work that God would do to fulfil the promise*).

3 Through the (*same*) faith (*that has been made flesh in Jesus*) we understand that the universe was (*shaped,*) formed (*and fashioned*) by the word of God, so that things which are seen were not made by the things which do appear (*but by the word of God that was from the beginning*).

4 (*Being persuaded*) by the same faith (*that was from the beginning and testified of the work which God would do in Christ, and the certainty of things not yet seen*) Abel offered unto God a far superior sacrifice than Cain, by which (*faith*) he obtained witness (*from God Himself*) that he was righteous (*in resting in His promise to provide Himself the lamb and decorate him in His life*), God testifying of (*the superiority of*) his gifts: that being persuaded by that faith though he being dead yet speaks.

5 (*Being persuaded*) by the same faith (*that was from the beginning and testified of the work which God would do in Christ, and the certainty of things not yet seen*) Enoch was translated (*from death to life*) not seeing (*God as the one who punishes with*) death (*but only seeing the reward of His life*); and was found no more, because God had taken him: because before his translation he bore the testimony (*of God*), by which he (*walked in agreement with and*) pleased God (*diligently seeking Him for the reward of His life*).

6 But without the faith (*contained in the word that was from the beginning and was made flesh in Jesus Christ*) it is

impossible that He find any pleasure (*seeing anyone drawback unto destruction*): for he that comes to God (*comes because he*) is (*fully*) persuaded that He (*already*) is (*pleased*), and that He is the rewarder (*of life and immortality and not the destroyer*) of them that diligently seek Him.

7 (*Being persuaded*) by the same faith (*that was from the beginning and testified of the work which God would do in Christ, and the certainty of things not yet seen*) Noah, (*having seen grace in God's eyes toward him and all mankind*) was warned by God concerning (*the revelation of*) things not yet seen, moved with reverential awe to prepare an ark (*that was pitched within and without according to God's instructions*) to the saving of his house; by which (*faith*) he condemned (*the life he could have in*) the world (*filled with labor and anguish, preaching to all people God's desire to preserve their lives from the destruction in the world*), and became an heir of the life that only comes from trusting in the work of God (*to fulfil His promise*).

8 (*Being persuaded*) by the same faith (*that was from the beginning and testified of the work which God would do in Christ, and the certainty of things not yet seen*) Abraham, when he was called to go out into a place which (*God promised that*) he (*and his seed*) should afterward receive for an inheritance, obeyed (*believing God*); and (*even though he had yet no child*) he went out, not knowing where he went.

9 (Being persuaded) by the same faith (*which was from the beginning and testified of the work which God would do in Christ, and the certainty of things not yet seen*) he dwelled in the land of promise, as a stranger in a strange country, dwelling in tents with Isaac and Jacob, who were the heirs along with him of the same promise:

10 For he looked for a city which had foundations (*not built with man's hands that could never see corruption*), whose builder and maker is God.

11 (*Being persuaded*) by the same faith (*which was from the beginning and testified of the work which God would do in Christ, and the certainty of things not yet seen*) Sara also

herself (*when she was old and barren*) received strength to conceive (*the promised*) seed and was able to deliver a child when she was past age, because she considered (*not the deadness of her womb but*) the One who had promised (*it as a certainty*) *trustworthy* (*to also be able to perform it*).

12 Therefore from (*the seed of*) one (*man*), and his own body (*impotent and*) as good as dead, were born so many as the stars of the sky in multitude, and as the sand of the seashore uncountable.

13 All these died in the same faith (*fully confident in the work that God said He would do*) but without having received the promises, only seeing them from afar and being persuaded of them and embraced them and confessed that they were like strangers in a strange land in the earth.

14 For they that say such things declare bluntly that they seek a country (*which they have yet come to*).

15 And truly, if they had been mindful of (*fondly remembering*) the country from where they came out of, they might have found an opportunity to return.

16 But instead they longed for a better country, one that is of a heavenly substance (*from above*): therefore, God is not ashamed to be surnamed their God (*the God of Abraham, Isaac, and Jacob*): for He has prepared (*just such*) a city for them.

17 (*Being persuaded*) by the same faith (*which was from the beginning and testified of the work which God would do in Christ, and the certainty of things not yet seen*) Abraham, when he was proven (*the faith manifested in his heart and he believed God*), offered up Isaac (*in the place where he saw God would provide Himself the lamb*): and he that had received the promises (*that through him and his seed he would become the father of many nations*) offered up his only begotten son (*believing the promise that God would preserve him and his seed eternally*).

18 Of whom it was said, that through Isaac will (*you and*) your seed be called (*blessed, the father of many nations*):

155

Hebrews 11

19 Considering that God (*who promised*) was also able to raise Isaac up, even from the dead: from where he also had received him (*from the deadness of his own body*) in the same way.

20 (*Being persuaded*) by the same faith (*which was from the beginning and testified of the work which God would do in Christ, and the certainty of things not yet seen*) Isaac blessed Jacob and Esau concerning (*good*) things to come (*not yet seen*).

21 (*Being persuaded*) by the same faith (*which was from the beginning and testified of the work which God would do in Christ, and the certainty of things not yet seen*) Jacob, when he was a dying, (*strengthened himself sitting upon his bed and*) blessed both the sons of Joseph; (*bowed his head*) and worshipped, leaning upon the top of his staff.

22 (*Being persuaded*) by the same faith (*which was from the beginning and testified of the work which God would do in Christ, and the certainty of things not yet seen*) Joseph, when he died, made mention of the departing of the children of Israel (*saying surely God will visit you, and will bring you out of this land to the land concerning which God promised to our fathers, Abraham, Isaac, and Jacob*); and (*for that reason*) gave instructions concerning his bones.

23 (*Being persuaded*) by the same faith (*which was from the beginning and testified of the work which God would do in Christ, and the certainty of things not yet seen*) Moses, when he was born, was hid (*and nourished up*) three months of his parents, because they saw he was an exceedingly beautiful child; and they were not afraid of the king's commandment.

24 (*Being persuaded*) by the same faith (*which was from the beginning and testified of the work which God would do in Christ, and the certainty of things not yet seen*) Moses, when he was grown (*to a full forty years old*), he refused to be called the son of Pharaoh's daughter;

25 Choosing rather to suffer affliction with (*his brethren*) the people of God, rather than enjoy the pleasures (*of self-preservation which perish*) that he could gather to himself (*in Egypt*) for a season;

26 Esteeming the reproach of Christ as greater riches than the treasures in Egypt: because he had the highest regard for and looked toward the (*the promise of the riches of God's life for*) reward.

27 (*Being persuaded*) by the same faith (*which was from the beginning and testified of the work which God would do in Christ, and the certainty of things not yet seen*) he left Egypt, not fearing the wrath of the king: for he persevered by seeing (*the faith of*) Him who was not yet seen.

28 By (*continually hearing this same*) faith he observed the Passover (*celebration of God's promise to provide Himself the lamb*), and the sprinkling of blood, so that the death which destroyed the firstborn could not touch them.

29 (*Being persuaded*) by the same faith they passed through the Red sea as if it were by dry ground: which the Egyptians attempting to do the same were drowned.

30 By (*this same*) faith (*which was from the beginning and testified of the work which God would do in Christ, and the certainty of things not yet seen*) the walls of Jericho fell down, having been encircled for seven days.

31 (*Being persuaded*) by the same faith (*which was from the beginning and testified of the work which God would do in Christ, and the certainty of things not yet seen*) the harlot Rahab did not perished with them who (*disobeyed, not allowing themselves to be persuaded that it is God who would preserve their life and*) believed not, when she had received the spies with peace.

32 And what more shall I say? for the time would fail me to tell of Gideon, and of Barak, and of Samson, and of Jephthah; of David also, and Samuel, and of all the prophets:

33 Who through the faith (*which was from the beginning and testified of the work which God would do in Christ, and the certainty of things not yet seen*) subdued kingdoms, administered justice, obtained promises, stopped the mouths of lions,

34 Quenched the power of fire, escaped the edge of the sword, were strengthened out of weakness, became mighty in battle, putting to flight the armies of the strangers.

35 Women received their dead raised to life again: and others were tortured (*in the world*), not accepting (*the world's*) deliverance; so that they might obtain a better (*incorruptible*) resurrection (*from the dead*):

36 And others received trials of (*torture inflicted*) mockings and scourging's, in addition to chains and imprisonment:

37 They were stoned, they were sawed in two, were tried, were slain with the sword: they wandered about in sheepskins and goatskins; being destitute, afflicted, tormented;

38 Of whom the world (*and the life it could offer them*) was not fitting (*to be compared to the life God promised to serve them with*): they wandered in deserts, and in mountains, and in huts and caves of the earth (*refusing any other life*).

39 And all these, having obtained a good report through (*the same word of*) faith (*that was from the beginning and was made flesh in Jesus Christ*), received not the promise:

40 God having foreseen (*that He would provide*) something better for us, and that they (*who saw the promises afar off*) would not be made perfect apart from us (*who have seen the promise made immortal flesh*).

Chapter 12

1 Therefore seeing we also are compassed about with so great a multitude of witnesses (*of the resurrection which is the promise of eternal life made immortal flesh*), let us lay aside every weight (*that the death in the world can bring*), and the temptation to serve ourselves with life (*and peace*) which does so easily entangle us, and (*seeing the certainty that His life and immortality will also manifest in us*) let us run with patience the race that is set before us,

2 Looking (*diligently*) unto Jesus, the originator and the perfecter of the faith (*made immortal flesh in the resurrection*); Who for the joy (*of the certainty of the life and immortality*) that

was set before Him endured the cross (*with patience, whereby He even said My cup runs over*), and considered not the shame (*of His nakedness as anything that could injure the life that the Father promised to clothe Him with*), and who is set down at the right hand of God (*in glorified immortal flesh and bone*).

3 For consider Him who endured such great contradiction from those blinded by death (*pertaining to*) the temptation to save His own life (*that came*) against Himself (*at the cross where He rested in the promise of the Father to clothe Him with His life and immortality*); so that (*when you are tempted to serve yourself with life*) you will (*rest in the certainty that He will also decorate you with that same life and*) not grow weary (*striving against death's accusation in your own strength*) whereby you faint in your minds.

4 (*Therefore consider the faith of Him because*) you have not yet resisted (*the temptation to preserve your own life*) unto (*the shedding of*) blood, struggling against the temptation (*to enlist your own members*) to preserve your life.

5 And you have forgotten the word which brings comfort and speaks to you as (*His*) children, My son, do not despise (*or neglect*) the correction of the Lord, or grow weary (*and lose heart*) when you are admonished of Him:

6 Because the Lord corrects (*all of*) the ones who He loves and scourges (*the death that speaks lies and erroneous doctrines contrary to His life in the heart of*) every son who He receives (*as His own*).

7 If you endure correction (*knowing that you are His beloved children*), (*you see that*) God is dealing with you as with sons; because what son is there where the father does not (*instruct and*) correct (*pertaining to life*)?

8 But if you reject (*His*) correction (*unto life*) which all have a share in (*and access to*), then you have made yourself bastards, and not sons (*by rejecting and disregarding the correction of the Father as His sons*).

9 Furthermore, we have had earthly fathers which corrected us, and we have had respect for them (*and their instruction*): how much more so should we stand (*in awe of, and diligently*

harkening unto Him, being) in subjection to the (*correction of*) the Father of the word of life (*made immortal flesh*) and live (*forever*).

10 For our earthly fathers corrected us for just a few days after their own pleasure but He (*has corrected our erroneous belief pertaining to the way unto life and immortality in Jesus Christ*) so that we might (*attain to our inheritance and*) share in the life which He has set apart for us (*to live forever in His life and likeness in immortal flesh, which life He set as the mark for our lives from the beginning*).

11 Now no correction at first seems to be joyous but can bring sorrow: but afterward (*if it is sown in peace, from above by the One who makes peace*) it yields the peaceful fruit (*that brings you rest*) which comes from (*beholding*) the (*holy*) life (*you were set apart for, in the hearts*) of those who (*after having grappled with an unconcealed heart*) are trained (*being persuaded*) by it.

12 Therefore lift up the hands which hang down, and the weakened knees;

13 And make straight paths for your feet (*which have gotten crooked*), so that which is lame would not be put out of joint; but that it would rather be healed (*and your life preserved forever*).

14 Pursue peace (*and His rest which brings tranquility*) with all men, and (*run your race with the patience and certainty of His*) holiness (*a life that has been sanctified from death*), for apart from (*seeing His desire to serve you with*) such (*a life will*) no man see the Lord (*with a pure heart*):

15 Looking diligently (*unto Jesus*) so that no man would (*grow weary striving against death in their own strength and thereby*) fail of the grace of God; so that no (*poisonous*) root of bitterness would spring up and trouble anyone (*with its erroneous doctrines*), and thereby be defiled (*in the bond of iniquity*);

16 So that there would not be any fornicator (*among you who goes and worships other gods*), or profane person (*whose heart is turned away from the Lord to serve their bellies with the*

works of their own hands), such as Esau, who for one morsel of meat sold his birthright (*the blessing of the first born*).

17 For you know how that afterward, when he (*wished he*) would (*still*) have inherited the blessing (*of the first born*), he was rejected: for he had no change in his heart (*regarding the reasonings by which he sold his birthright, thinking instead that he was still due the blessing*), (*and was denied*) though he sought it carefully with tears.

18 For you are not come to the mount that might be touched (*as those who would not draw near when He spoke on earth*) and which (*mountain*) burned with fire, nor unto the thick cloud (*that concealed with*) blackness and darkness and thunder (*shaking the earth*),

19 And to the sound of a trumpet (*which signaled they could approach*), and the voice of (*His*) words, which voice they that heard begged (*Moses imploring him*) that the word should not be spoken to them anymore (*for fear that they would die*):

20 For they could not endure (*the temptation to preserve their own lives but withdrew because of the fear that death brought to their hearts in*) that which was commanded: (*which said*) "if so much as a beast touch the mountain, it will be stoned or shot through with a dart (*it will not live*): (*but when the trumpet sounded long, they will approach the mount*):"

21 And so dreadful was the appearance, that (*even*) Moses (*who did draw near the mount*) said, I exceedingly fear and tremble:

22 But you are come unto mount Zion (*from where the word of the Lord has gone forth again from heaven*), and unto the city of the living God, the heavenly Jerusalem (*that abides forever*), and to an innumerable multitude of angels,

23 To the general assembly and church of (*Jesus Christ*) the firstborn (*from the dead*), whose names are written in heaven, and to God the Judge of all, and to the spirits of just men (*whose consciences have been purged from death*) made perfect (*reserved unto the same inheritance incorruptible*),

24 And to Jesus Christ (*the second Adam and the Lord from heaven*) the mediator of the new covenant, and to the blood of

161

sprinkling (*which purges our conscience from death*), that speaks (*saying death that has been conquered and justice has been served*) a more excellent thing than (*the blood*) of Abel (*which cried out for justice from the ground*).

25 See that you do not refuse (*to hear*) Him that speaks (*His judgment unto life*). For if they who refused (*to hear*) Him withdrew when He spoke on earth, much more will we also drawback, if we turn away from (*hearing the faith of*) Him that speaks from heaven:

26 Whose voice at that time shook the earth: but now He has promised, saying, yet once more I will shake not only the earth, but also heaven (*the sea and the dry land*).

27 And (*the same spirit of faith contained in*) this word, (*which He has spoken*) yet once more (*in Christ*), signifies the removing of those things which (*will pass away that*) are shaken, as in (*the purifying by fire*) the things that are created, so that those things which cannot (*ever be moved or*) be shaken may remain (*incorruptible, baptized in the fire of His life*).

28 Therefore, (*seeing as*) we are (*come to and are*) receiving a kingdom (*the heavenly Jerusalem that abides forever*) which cannot ever be moved (*or shaken*), let us receive (*His*) grace (*and strength*). Whereby we rest in Him (*and His everlasting-kindness to serve us with all the fruit of His life unto immortality in our flesh*), so that we may worship God in a way well pleasing to Him, with all reverence and godly fear (*and awe of Him as the only One who can serve us with that life*).

29 Because our God is a consuming fire (*even a jealous God who is passionate over our lives, as a Father who desires to serve His children with the only life He saw fitting for us from the beginning*).

Chapter 13

1 Let brotherly love (*kindness and affection*) continue (*to abide in you, as you abide in Him, where you honor one another, for we are all members of one body*).

2 And do not be forgetful to (*share this*) love and be generous with strangers (*even to the least of these*): for in doing so some have entertained messengers (*of the Lord*) without knowing it.

3 Remember those who are in bonds, as bound with them (*as members of the same body*); and them which suffer adversity (*and are mistreated*), because you yourselves are also in the body.

4 Marriage is honorable (*precious and to be esteemed*) by all (*who take part in it*), and the (*marriage*) bed is (*pure and*) undefiled: but fornicators and adulterers God judges (*that they trespass against their own body*).

5 Let your way of life be free from the love of money (*always lusting for more*); but be satisfied with such things as you have: for (*all that He has is yours and*) He Himself has said, I will never leave you, nor forsake you.

6 So that we may boldly say, The Lord is my (*shepherd, my ever present*) helper (*in my time of need, who rescues my life from destruction*), so that I will not fear what man will do to me.

7 Be mindful of those which have the rule over you, who have spoken to you the word of God: of whom, observing closely the end of their way of life; follow the faith (*of Jesus Christ*).

8 Jesus Christ the same yesterday, and today, and forever.

9 Do not be carried (*and tossed*) about with various and strange doctrines (*which are outside of the faith of Jesus Christ*). For it is good that the heart be established (*and to find its strength only*) in (*the*) grace (*and strength of the Lord Jesus*), not with food rituals (*and restrictions*) which have not profited those who have been occupied with them (*because those things have no ability to strengthen them unto the life and immortality of God*).

10 We have an altar (*upon which God has provided Himself the lamb*), from which they have no right to eat (*seeing as they*) which serve the tabernacle (*do so upon the altar made with man's hands providing themselves a lamb*).

11 For the bodies of those beasts, whose blood is brought into the sanctuary by the high priest for the trespasses of the

people, (*neither the people nor the priests may eat thereof but*) are burned outside the camp (*the Holy Spirit signifying that the way to the holiest place was not manifest upon the altar made with man's hands*).

12 Therefore Jesus also, that He might sanctify the people (*from death*) with His own blood, suffered (*death in the flesh*) outside the gate.

13 Therefore let us go forth to Him outside the camp, (*seeing as we also are*) bearing the (*same*) reproach as Him (*of death in our flesh; looking unto the faith of Jesus Christ, where we find the strength for our hearts to disesteem the shame the death in the world can bring us as anything that can injure the life that the Father promised to clothe us with, seeing the joy and certainty of the life which manifested in Him in immortal flesh in the resurrection*).

14 For (*we are strangers*) here (*in a world filled with death and corruption*) having no continuing city (*that will abide forever*), but we seek (*the*) one to come (*knowing that we are citizens of a heavenly country; that is under the reign of an indestructible life*).

15 By (*looking unto and calling upon*) Him therefore let us continually offer the sacrifice of praise to God, which is (*the only sacrifice He ever desired*), the fruit of (*His life that the Spirit brings to*) our lips (*whereby we cry Abba Father*) giving thanks to (*and calling upon*) His name (*in perfect praise*).

16 And do not forget to do good (*to those in need*) and to share (*your substance with others as well as communicate the hope that you have in you*): for with such sacrifices God is well pleased.

17 Listen carefully to (*and allow yourself to be persuaded by*) those who (*have spoken the word of God to you and*) have rule over you (*leading you toward the faith of Jesus Christ*) and submit yourselves (*to their counsel in the Lord*): for they watch for your souls as ones that must deliver a word (*as if about their very own lives, expressing the thoughts of the Father through the Spirit*), so that they may do it with joy, and not

groaning (*within themselves in anger or frustration*): because that is unprofitable for you.

18 Pray for us (*and our ministry*): for we are persuaded we have a good conscience (*in Christ*), in all these things desiring to live honestly.

19 But I urge you even more abundantly to pray for me, so that I may be restored (*and return*) to you sooner.

20 Now the God of peace (*fill you with hope*), who has brought again from the dead our Lord Jesus, that great Shepherd of the sheep, through the blood of the everlasting covenant (*that is without end*),

21 Make you perfect (*as He is perfect, sanctified from death*) unto every good work (*which work He has beforehand prepared for you to walk in*) to walk in His will (*and the justice of His incorruptible life*), working in you that which is well pleasing in His sight (*unto His same life and immortality in your flesh*), through Jesus Christ; to whom be glory for ever and ever. Amen.

22 And I implore you, brethren, to listen closely (*to consider*) this word of exhortation (*and comfort so that you may endure any and all contradiction*): for I have written a letter to you in few words.

23 Know that our brother Timothy is set at liberty; with whom, if he comes shortly, I will see you as well.

24 Salute all of them that have the rule over you, and all the saints. They of Italy salute you.

25 The grace (*of our Lord Jesus*) be with you all. Amen.

The General Epistle of

JAMES

The Faith Translation

Chapter 1

1 James, a bondservant (*devoted to and in the love*) of God and of the Lord Jesus Christ, to the twelve tribes which are scattered across the nations, rejoice.

2 My brethren, consider (*and esteem above all things*) the faith (*of Him*) with all joy when you fall into (*and are surrounded by*) various temptations;

3 Knowing this, that this faith which works in you (*to persuade you of the work which God has already done to overcome all temptation*) is (*tried and*) proven to produce (*the fruit of*) patience.

4 And allow that patience to have her perfect work, so that you may be perfect and complete, (*being fully persuaded that you do not need to care for your own life, but where you rest that He has given you all things pertaining to life and Godlikeness*) where you lack no good thing.

5 But if any of you lack wisdom let him look to God, the One who has given (*the same measure of faith*) to all men and gives generously and without (*accusation or*) finding fault (*or respect of persons*), and it will be given him.

6 But let him that asks (*for wisdom*) be (*fully persuaded that it is found*) in the faith, not vacillating (*and fornicating being intimate with his own imaginations and the wisdom in the world*). For he who does that is unstable (*and uncertain, not being persuaded by the faith and*) is like a wave of the sea that can be blown and tossed back and forth by the wind.

7 For truly the man (*looking to his own imaginations and the way in the world*) ought not think that he will receive anything from the Lord (*in his own strength and wisdom*).

8 A double minded man (*who being a forgetful hearer of the faith instead looks to the way in the world which stands opposed to the wisdom and knowledge of God and does not continue in the faith of Jesus Christ*) is unstable in all his ways.

9 Let the brother who (*being poor in spirit*) does not think more highly of himself than he should (*seeing his inability to preserve his own life eternally*) rejoice (*in the faith of Jesus*

James 1

Christ) that he is exalted (*unto the life and immortality of God apart from his own strength*):

10 But let the man rich (*in worldly goods*), (*rejoice*) in that he is brought low (*in humility*): seeing that (*his corruptible flesh is*) like the flower of the grass so will he pass away (*apart from the strength of God to preserve him unto life and immortality in his flesh*).

11 For the sun is no sooner risen with its burning heat and it withers the grass, and the flower of it falls (*to the ground*), and the beauty of its appearance perishes: so also, will the rich man fade away by his own ways (*and strength to preserve his dying flesh*).

12 Blessed is the man who (*through the faith of Jesus Christ*) endures (*with patience the*) temptation (*brought by death*): for when he is tried (*he is strengthened thereby*), he will receive the crown of life, which the Lord has promised (*from the beginning*) to all of them that love Him.

13 Let no man say when he is tempted (*by death*), I am tempted of God: for God (*who has no death in Him*) can (*therefore*) not be tempted with evil (*to try and preserve His own life, seeing as He already possesses an incorruptible life*), neither does He tempt any man (*to do that, because He has already promised to serve them with His life*):

14 But every man is tempted (*by death and not by God*), when he is drawn away of his own lust (*for life*), and enticed (*to take it by force, by the strength of his own hand*).

15 Then when (*their*) lust (*for life by their own works*) has conceived (*in their heart*), it brings forth (*the sting of death which is*) iniquity: and iniquity, when it is finished, brings forth death.

16 Do not be misled (*in error*), my beloved brethren.

17 Every good gift and every perfect gift (*originates and*) is from above (*from the word that was from the beginning*) and comes down from the Father of lights, with whom there is no variableness, (*the same yesterday, today and forever*), neither any shadow from His turning.

18 Of His own purpose (*and desire*) begat He us with the word of truth (*that was from the beginning and was made immortal flesh in the resurrection of Jesus Christ*), so that we should be a kind of firstfruits of His creatures (*the beginning of the creation of God*).

19 Therefore, (*knowing this*) my beloved brethren, let every man be swift to hear (*and hearken diligently to that word of truth He has spoken*), slow to speak, slow to wrath:

20 For the wrath of man does not produce (*or help bring forth*) the justice of God (*to appear in the life and immortality which God has set apart for you from the beginning*).

21 Therefore lay aside all filthiness (*which is idolatry, making flesh your arm and your god*) and the abundance of (*labor and annoyances that*) wickedness (*will bring to you*) and receive with meekness the word implanted (*into your heart, where you no longer try to take the kingdom by force but rest in God to give it to you as a gift*), which (*word*) is able to save your souls (*from perishing in the grave*).

22 But be doers of the word (*by continuing in the work of looking to the One who promised, seeing He is also able to perform it to completion*), and not only hearers, deceiving yourselves (*in your own hearts*).

23 For if anyone is a hearer of the word and not a doer, he is like a man who beholds his natural face in a mirror:

24 For he views himself and goes away and immediately forgets what likeness he is.

25 But whoever looks into the perfect law of liberty (*at the word of promise made immortal flesh in the resurrection of Jesus Christ*) and continues (*to do the work of resting in the promise*) therein, he is not a forgetful hearer but a doer of the work (*of continuing in that word*), this man will be blessed in his deed.

26 If any man among you thinks (*himself*) to be religious (*in his fear and worship of God*) but (*what he believes in his heart*) does not (*and is unable to*) curb his tongue (*from speaking evil*), but rather deceives his own heart, this man's religion is worthless.

27 Pure and undefiled religion comes from God the Father and is this; (*to see that the Father has come in Jesus Christ*) To visit the fatherless and widows in their affliction (*of death*), and (*being persuaded by and continuing in this word that the Father has poured out His life for us is one able*) to keep himself (*and his tongue*) unspotted from (*the corruption that is in*) the world (*through the lust of the flesh for life*).

Chapter 2

1 My brethren, regard not the faith of our Lord Jesus Christ, the Lord of glory, to have (*any partiality or*) respect of persons.
2 For if a man comes into your assembly with a gold ring, in splendid apparel, and a poor man comes in also with shabby (*or filthy*) clothing;
3 And you have respect for (*and look upon*) him that wears the splendid apparel (*with partiality*) saying to him, sit here in the place of honor; and you say to the poor man (*looking upon him as beneath you*), stand over there or sit here under my footrest (*in the place of dishonor*):
4 Are you not then judging (*with partiality between the two*) within your own hearts and have you not made yourselves out to be judges with evil (*envious and harassing*) thoughts (*judging unjustly according to appearances and not righteously by the faith of Jesus Christ*)?
5 Listen, my beloved brethren, has not God chosen the poor (*in spirit*) in this world (*those who see they have no ability to serve themselves with His life and immortality to be*) made rich in the faith (*of Jesus Christ*) and heirs of (*God and*) the kingdom which He has promised (*from the beginning*) to them that love Him?
6 But you have dishonored (*and rejected*) the (*ones who the world esteems as*) poor. Do not rich men oppress you, and drag you (*into court*) before judge's seats?
7 Do they not slander the name (*of Christ Jesus our Lord*) that is worthy of all honor (*and glory*) by which (*name*) you are called (*unto the same honor and glory*)?

8 If you actually fulfil the royal (*chief*) law outwardly according to the scripture, "You will love your neighbor as yourself," you do well:

9 But if you have respect (*and partiality*) of persons (*in your heart*), you do trespass (*falling short of the spirit contained in the law, that declares that royal life which the Father has promised to serve you with*) and you will judge (*yourself*) by the law as transgressors (*because you are looking to your own strength instead of continuing to do the work of resting in Him to give you His blessing and life as an inheritance*).

10 For the one who truly desires to keep the whole law, and yet stumbles in one point (*is not continuing in the work of resting in the perfect law of liberty*), he is bound by (*judging and condemning himself of*) all.

11 For the One that said, you will not commit adultery, said also, you will not kill. Now if you do not commit adultery, but you kill, you have become a transgressor (*and you will judge yourself guilty*) of the (*whole*) law.

12 So speak and so continue to do the work (*of resting in the promise*), as those who will be judged (*justly*) by the perfect law of liberty (*which is the word of promise made immortal flesh in the bodily resurrection of Jesus Christ*).

13 For he who has a judgment (*in his heart that is*) apart from (*continuing to rest in the*) mercy (*and love of the Father to serve him with His blessing and life as a gift*), that judgment will not produce mercy (*in his heart but will condemn him*); (*however, the heart of the one who continues resting in*) His judgment boasts (*loudly*) of (*His*) mercy.

14 My brethren, what does it profit a man that although he may say I have faith, does not do (*the one thing needful, which is*) the work, (*of looking to the faith of Jesus Christ to father his life, which provides him everything that he needs to partake of His life and Godlikeness*)? Is that faith alone (*apart from doing the work of allowing himself to be persuaded by it*) able to save him (*from the death and calamity in the world and raise him from the grave immortal*)?

James 2

15 If a brother or sister be naked, destitute (*and lacking*) of daily food,

16 And one of you say to them, go in peace, be warmed and filled (*with food*); nevertheless, you do not give them the things which are needful to the body; what does it profit (*them in their lack of food and clothing*)?

17 Even so (*saying I have*) the faith, apart from the work (*of allowing your heart to be persuaded by the faith of Jesus Christ, where you see with certainty that the Father of the Word of life has provided you all that is needful for you to partake of His indestructible life*) is (*such a faith*) dead, being alone.

18 But someone might say you have faith, and I have works: (*but*) show me (*how*) the faith that you have (*is able to save you from the corruption and death in the world*) apart from the work (*of being persuaded by the Father's good work; the word that was made immortal flesh in the resurrection of Jesus Christ*), and I will show you the faith (*that dwells*) in my heart by my work (*which is to do the work of continuing to look to the certainty contained in that word made immortal flesh whereby I rest from my own works to justify myself unto His life and immortality*).

19 You believe that there is one God; you do well: the devils also believe, and tremble.

20 But do you desire to know (*the truth*), O (*foolish*) vain man, that (*such a*) faith (*by itself*) without the work (*of allowing yourself to be persuaded that you do not need to preserve your own life*) is dead (*and void of power*)?

21 Was not Abraham our father justified (*as the father of many nations*) by (*continuing in*) the work (*of being persuaded that the One who promised was also able to perform it*), when he had offered Isaac his son (*through whom the seed would come*) upon the altar?

22 Do you see how the faith (*that was made immortal flesh in the resurrection of Jesus*) shaped his work, and through the work (*of being persuaded that death could not prevent God from preserving the promise seed eternally*) was the faith made perfect (*in Abraham*)?

23 And the scripture was fulfilled which said, Abraham believed God (*considering not the weakness contained in his dying flesh but he rejoiced in seeing Jesus day and the strength that was revealed in the Father's hand in His resurrection from the dead*), and (*the faith that dwelled in his heart*) was proven to be the thing (*whereby he would appear*) unto the life (*and immortality*) of God: and he was fully persuaded by God's invitation (*considering Him*) to be his friend.

24 You see then that it is by (*continuing in*) the work (*of looking to and being persuaded by the word the Father has spoken and was made immortal flesh in Jesus that*) a man is justified (*from death's accusation and will appear in His life and immortality*), and not by faith alone.

25 Likewise also was not Rahab the harlot justified by the work (*of being persuaded*), when (*destruction was going to come to her house*) she (*having heard the faith through the children of Israel when they were in Egypt, was not a forgetful hearer but remembered and believed that the power for her to overcome this destruction is found in the strength of God's hands and not her own so that when she*) had received the messengers, and sent them out another way (*she hung a scarlet thread outside her window which declared her testimony that God will cause death to pass over me by the strength of His hand by the blood of His lamb*)?

26 For just as the body without the spirit is (*subject to*) death, so is the faith apart from the work (*of continuing to allowing yourself to be persuaded*) dead (*being powerless to preserve your life from the death and corruption in the world*).

Chapter 3

1 My brothers, there are not many (*desiring to be*) teachers knowing that (*as we judge*) we will receive greater judgment (*of men and ourselves*).

2 For in many ways we all stumble. (*However*) if any man does not stumble in his words, the same is a perfect man, because

James 3

(*by the faith that dwells in his heart*) he is also able to guide his (*tongue and therefore his*) whole body.

3 Now if we put bits in the horses' mouths, so that they may obey us; we are able to turn about (*and guide*) their whole body.

4 Behold, also the ships, which though they are so great (*in size*), and are driven of strong winds, yet they are turned about by a very small rudder, wherever the one steering so desires.

5 Likewise also the tongue is a small member (*of the body*) which boasts in great (*strength and lofty*) things. Behold, how great a forest fire, a small fire, can kindle.

6 And (*in the same way*) the tongue is a fire, a world (*full*) of iniquity: so is the tongue among all our (*bodies*) members, that it (*is able to*) defile (*polluting*) the whole body and sets on fire (*steering*) the (*natural*) wheel of life (*toward destruction*); and is set on fire by hell (*itself*).

7 For every kind of beast, and bird, and creeping things, and things in the sea, are tamable, and have been tamed (*and subdued*) by mankind:

8 But the tongue (*apart from the faith and grace of God dwelling in the heart*) can no man tame; it is an unstable evil (*destructive and desperately wicked*), (*and when it speaks from a deceitful heart*) full of deadly poison (*from the serpent*).

9 With the tongue we bless the Lord, and the Father; and with the same (*tongue*) we curse men, those (*who were predestined*) to be made unto the likeness of God.

10 Out of the same mouth proceeds (*life and death*) praise and cursing (*condemning words*). My brethren, these things should not be so.

11 Does a fountain send forth from the same place sweet water and bitter?

12 Can the fig tree bear olive berries? My brethren, or a grapevine, figs? so also can a fountain not produce both salt water and fresh.

13 Who among you (*would say that they*) are wise and skilled with knowledge? let him show out of (*the abundance of his heart*) the good life that it works (*in his heart and that it is able*)

174

to produce the way that leads to life (*and peace*) with (*humility and*) meekness of wisdom.

14 But if you have bitter jealousy and strife (*conflict and contradiction that comes from*) within your hearts, in that you should not boast (*esteeming that wisdom, whereby you are deceived*) and lie against the truth (*that is against the true wisdom of God*).

15 This wisdom does not come from above but (*from below and*) is earthly, carnal, (*and proceeds from*) the doctrines of demons.

16 For where there is jealousy and strife, there is confusion (*instability*) and every evil (*laborious and molesting*) work (*that the flesh can produce*).

17 But the wisdom that is (*from Christ*) from above is first pure (*full of the life and power of God, uncontaminated, unable to ever cause harm*), then peaceable (*working in the heart the peace and rest that it has always longed for, free from every tormenting labor*), gentle, light and easy to be persuaded by, full of (*His*) mercy (*which is able to relieve all our suffering from the death and corruption in the world*) and (*it yields*) all the good fruit (*of His life*), without partiality (*or respect of persons*), genuine (*unpolluted and undisguised*) free from any hypocrisy (*or any hidden agendas*).

18 Now (*when*) the fruit of righteousness is sown in peace by those (*the peacemakers*) it brings peace (*and reaps mercy*).

Chapter 4

1 From where do disputes, (*strife*) and fighting come from among you? Do they not come from (*and originate with*) the passions that war in your members (*to preserve your lives from the death and corruption in the world*)?

2 You lust (*for life and peace*) and you have not, you kill, desiring to gain it but you cannot obtain it: you fight and war, yet you have not (*peace or rest*), because you ask not.

3 You ask and receive not (*the life and peace your heart truly desires*), because you ask amiss (*thinking you can gain it from*

the world) so that you may spend it upon your lusts (*whereby you are continually animated by the death and corruption in the world*).

4 You adulterers and adulteresses, do you not know that (*your Maker is your husband and*) the friendship (*and affection*) of the world (*which can only serve you with death*) is (*contrary to and*) hostile toward (*the judgment of*) God (*to serve you with His indestructible life*)? therefore, whoever will be a friend of the world has set themselves contrary to (*the judgment of*) God.

5 Do you think that the scripture says in vain, Thc Spirit that (*passionately*) desires to dwell in us, jealously longs to have us (*as His own*)?

6 But (*to the humble*) He gives more grace. Therefore, the scripture says God resists (*the way of*) the proud (*who are lifted up in their heart, looking to their own strength, to do, to get and to have*) but gives grace to the humble (*who being poor in spirit, look only to God and His strength*).

7 Submit yourselves therefore (*in subjection*) to (*the strength of*) God (*who in Christ has already stood in the face of death's accusation for us all*), (*so that you are able to*) resist the (*temptation to justify yourself brought by that slanderous*) accuser (*the devil, which says that because of death you are not the children of God*), and death (*and its accusation*) will flee from you.

8 Draw near to God and He will draw near to you. Cleanse your hands (*from death*) you fornicators (*who being intimate with the works thereof, serve yourself with death*); and (*instead look to the work which God has done in Christ to*) purify your hearts (*from death's influence*), you double minded.

9 (*And seeing the complete wretchedness of your own ability to exalt yourself to life*) be afflicted, mourn and weep: let your laughter be turned to sorrow, and your joy to gloom.

10 Humble yourselves (*taking no thought for the preservation of your own life*) in the sight of the Lord, and He will exalt you (*raising you up to an indestructible life which has no end*).

11 Do not speak poorly of (*and backbite*) one another, brethren. He that speaks against (*and slanders*) his brother and judges (*himself better than*) his brother, (*actually*) speaks against the law (*which says love your brother*) and judges the law: but if you judge (*yourself higher than*) the law, you are not a doer of the law, but (*have set yourself up as*) a judge.

12 There is One Lawgiver (*and One Judge of all*), The One Who is able to (*both*) save (*and preserve your life forever from destruction*) and to destroy (*the enemy death*): who are you (*that can do neither*) that judges one another?

13 Hear now, those of you who say, today or tomorrow we will go into this city and spend a year there and will trade and will make a gain,

14 Who (*boast of tomorrow and*) do not even know what will be on the next day. (*Have you not considered*) what is (*the nature of*) this life of yours? Is it not but a vapor that appears for a short time and then vanishes away?

15 And for that reason, you ought to say (*instead*), If the Lord is willing, we will live and do this or that.

16 But (*as it stands*) now you rejoice in (*yourselves and in*) your boasting (*of the life you can build yourself*): all such boasting is evil (*not born from above but filled with labors and annoyances*).

17 Therefore, to him that knows to obey (*the*) good (*and perfect and praiseworthy life, which is only found in Christ, the Word of life made immortal flesh*) and he does not (*submit himself to*) obey that good (*and perfect law of liberty*), to him it is transgression.

Chapter 5

1 Hear now, you men who trust in riches, weep, and howl for your (*grief and the*) miseries (*and destruction*) that are sure to come upon you.

2 Your riches are corrupted (*and decayed*), and your garments are (*already*) motheaten (*and on the verge of perishing*).

James 5

3 Your gold and silver are tarnished; and their rust will be a witness against you and will eat the (*very*) flesh (*you are trying to preserve*) as if it were fire. You have gathered together (*storing up*) for yourself (*corruptible*) treasures that (*decay and*) will perish on the last day.

4 Behold, the wage of the workers you have used to harvest your fields, which wage you have kept back (*for yourself*), and the cries (*of injustice*) from those who have harvested, have entered into the ears of the Lord of Host.

5 You have lived in luxury on the earth and have been self-indulgent; you have fattened your heart and (*the innermost parts of*) your bellies (*in order to satisfy your desire for life through the riches of the world*), like (*sheep destined*) for the day of slaughter.

6 You have condemned and put to death the righteous (*who only look to God and His grace to preserve their lives from destruction*) and they did not resist you.

7 Therefore be patient, brethren, unto the coming of the Lord (*Jesus*). Behold, the husbandman (*the Father of all*) waits for the precious fruit of the earth, and has long patience for the harvest thereof, until (*the fullness of time when*) he will receive (*to Himself the fruit of*) the early and latter rain (*from the pouring out of His Spirit unto the resurrection of the dead in a glorified earth*).

8 (*Therefore*), you also may be patient; having your hearts established (*in the faith and strengthened by the sure hope of the gospel*): for the coming (*day*) of the Lord (*where He will join all things in heaven and earth to Himself as One*) draws closer.

9 Do not murmur (*within yourselves, judging*) one against another, brethren, so that you will not (*judge and*) condemn yourselves (*of the same thing*): behold (*instead*) the (*One*) Judge (*who holds the only true judgment, He is near and even*) stands before the door.

10 Take (*those things which were set forth as*) an example my brethren, (*considering*) the suffering of affliction and patience of the prophets who spoke in the name of the Lord.

11 Behold, we consider them blessed which endured (*affliction*). You have heard of the patience of Job and have seen the end of the Lord; that the Lord is (*filled with and*) moved by compassion (*at our suffering of affliction at the hands of death*) and (*desires*) with (*His*) tender mercy (*to relieve us from our suffering*).

12 But above all things, my brethren, do not swear (*an oath*), by (*invoking*) heaven (*upon your own lust for it is God's throne*), or by the earth (*for it is His footstool*), or by making any other oath (*of your own*): but (*as you look to and are persuaded by Him*) let your yes be a simple yes; and your no, be a simple no (*for anything else comes not from the wisdom above*); so that you do not (*condemn yourselves and thereby*) fall under (*the weight of your own*) judgment.

13 Is there any among you suffering hardships (*and afflictions*)? let him pray (*to the Father who is able to strengthen him so that he may endure*). Is there anyone cheerful? let him sing praises.

14 Is there any (*feeling*) weak (*and without strength*) among you? Let him call for those mature in the faith within the church; and let them pray (*declaring the faith*) over him, (*which is able to*) anoint him with (*the*) oil (*only the Spirit can give*) in the name of the Lord:

15 And the prayer that imparts faith (*to the hearer*) will save (*and bring rest to*) the one who is weary (*exhausted and without strength*) and the Lord will raise him up (*strengthening him in the inner man*) and if he has (*been overtaken by*) any offenses (*that come from self-preservation*), they will be (*pacified and*) sent away from him.

16 Therefore (*seeing as we all can be tempted to preserve our lives from the corruption and death in the world*), (*let us*) confess our faults to one another and pray (*declaring the faith*) over one another so that you may be healed (*and find the rest your heart truly desires*). The prayer of a righteous man is (*one that sees that only the Father can serve with the righteousness our hearts have ever longed for and that it is His good pleasure to do so*), (*this is*) the effective prayer because it is (*full of*

179

power) able to prevail over the death and corruption in the world and strengthen one unto that life.

17 Elias was a (*righteous*) man with a passionate desire for life just as we are (*who because of like infirmities was subject to all the same temptations death can bring*), and he (*earnestly*) prayed a prayer (*to the only living God whom he revered*) that it might not rain: and it did not rain on the earth for a space of three years and six months.

18 And he prayed again, and the (*Lord from*) heaven gave the rain and the earth brought forth her fruit (*upon the formerly dry ground*).

19 Brethren, if anyone among you wanders from the truth, and someone (*comes alongside them with the faith of our Lord Jesus and it*) turns their hearts back (*to the truth*);

20 Let it be known, that (*the Spirit of the Lord is*) the One (*who rains from heaven*) that turns (*the heart of*) the transgressor from the error of his way (*unto life*), saving a soul from (*perishing in the second*) death and (*fully persuading them that their death has been sent away*) will cover a multitude of offenses (*formerly brought by the body of death*).

The First Epistle of

PETER

The Faith Translation

Chapter 1

1 Peter, an apostle of Jesus Christ, to the (*partakers of eternal salvation*) scattered (*as strangers in strange lands*) throughout Pont'us, Ga-la'tia, Cap-pa-do'ci-a, A'sia, and Bi-thyn'i-a,

2 Set apart (*to partake of His life and immortality*) according to the determined purpose (*and promise*) of God the Father (*since before the world began*), who through the sanctification of the Spirit (*may be conformed*) to His image, allowing themselves to be persuaded and their conscience purged (*from the fear of death*) by the sprinkling of the blood (*that ran out*) of Jesus Christ: By whom (*His*) Grace (*persuades us of the certainty of His life*), and where (*His*) peace, (*and rest*) will be multiplied (*unto you*).

3 Blessed be the God and Father of our Lord Jesus Christ, who (*by His strength alone and*) according to His lovingkindness and abundant mercy has rescued us (*from the dead*) recreating us in Christ again to a sure hope (*of the same life and likeness to be revealed in us*) that lives in immortal flesh and bone (*at the Father's right hand*) by the (*bodily*) resurrection of Jesus Christ from the dead,

4 To the (*same*) inheritance (*revealed in Him*) incorruptible, indestructible, and undefiled (*by blood*), that (*can never die, perish*) or fade away, reserved (*in Christ at the Father's right hand*) in heaven for you,

5 Who are kept (*in the certainty of Him*) by the power of God through (*the*) faith (*revealed in Jesus Christ*) to (*bring the same life and*) salvation (*in the redemption of our bodies*) prepared and ready to be revealed (*in His return*) on the last day (*of death in the earth*).

6 In this (*living hope*) do you greatly rejoice, although now it might be necessary for a short while that you are grieved (*in your body*) with various temptations:

7 (*Count it all joy*) that the trying of your faith (*is sure, because it is found in the testimony of Jesus Christ, who having already stood in the face of all temptation for us, made death bow down*), which (*testimony*) is much more precious than that of gold that perishes, and though we (*who bear His testimony*) be

tried with fire, that we might be found (*abiding in Him*) to praise and honor and glory at the appearing of Jesus Christ:

8 Whom having not seen (*Him*), you love (*Him*); in whom, even though you do not now see Him, yet you believe (*in the testimony He has given of you*), and you rejoice with a joy (*that is*) unspeakable and full of glory:

9 Receiving (*His same just reward in your body*) the end of your faith, even the salvation of your entire being (*made immortal*).

10 Of this salvation the prophets have desired and searched (*out*) diligently, who prophesied about the grace that would come to you (*in Christ*):

11 Inquiring as to what, or what manner of time the Spirit of Christ, which (*spoke*) in (*and through*) them was showing them, when they testified beforehand (*about*) the sufferings of Christ, and the glory that would follow.

12 To whom it was revealed that they were not ministering these things to themselves but to us, the things which are now reported to you by (*me and*) those who have preached the gospel to you with the Holy Ghost sent down from heaven; which things (*pertaining to salvation*) even the angels desire to look into.

13 Therefore, be prepared, ready and alert, having a sound mind (*that is not intoxicated by the corruption in the world*), but (*abiding in the sure*) hope to the end (*waiting patiently*) for the grace (*wherein you will receive strength*) that is to be brought to you at the revelation of Jesus Christ;

14 Like little children, you can go to rest (*trusting in the Father to care for your life, fully reliant upon Him*), no longer having to establish your own life according to (*the world's corrupt wisdom*) where you formerly lusted for life (*in vain*) in your ignorance.

15 But just as the One who has (*surnamed*) you (*His son*) is holy (*having set you apart to be fathered with His life*), so (*will you as His children*) be holy (*set apart to be fathered by Him*) in all manner of life (*and Godlikeness*);

1 Peter 1

16 Because it is written, you will be holy (*set apart unto Me and by Me, for you are My portion*) because I AM holy (*and My heart is set apart unto you*).

17 And if you call upon the Father (*for the incorruptible life He has set you apart for*), the One who impartially judges according (*whether or not*) the quality of a man's work be perishable, so will you pass the time of living as a stranger in a strange land, esteeming Him (*and His incorruptible work*):

18 Because knowing this, you know that you were not released from the bondage of death by corruptible things, such as silver and gold, from that life where you formerly labored in vain (*never finding rest*) living by the traditions established by your fathers (*and not God*).

19 But (*you were released from the reign of death*) with the precious blood (*that ran out*) of Christ, (*the only life that could measure the true value of your own*), like that of an (*innocent*) lamb without blemish (*blameless*) and without spot (*unstained by death*):

20 (*Christ*) who truly was foreordained (*the substance and the promise of eternal life*) before the foundation of the world (*before death entered*), but was revealed in (*immortal flesh*) in these last times for you (*to behold the promise in immortal flesh and bone*),

21 (*Christ*) who by Him do (*you*) believe in God (*as your Father*), who raised Him up from the dead, and gave Him glory; so that your faith and hope might (*rest*) in God (*for the certainty of the same life*).

22 Seeing you have purified your hearts, being persuaded of the truth through the Spirit of life (*that you behold in Christ, which gives birth to a*) sincere love for the brethren, so that (*abiding in His life*) you would love one another passionately and with a pure heart:

23 Being born again from above (*by the Spirit of God*), not from corruptible seed (*of the flesh*), but of incorruptible (*of the Spirit*), by (*Christ*) the word of God, which lives and abides forever.

24 Because all flesh is like grass, and all the glory that a man (*could bring forth in himself*) is like the flower of grass. The grass withers, and the flower thereof fades away:

25 But the word of the Lord (*which God has spoken about you in Christ*) endures forever (*in immortal flesh and bone at the Father's right hand*). And this is the word (*that contains the power of His indestructible life*) which by the gospel (*of Jesus Christ*) is preached to you.

Chapter 2

1 Having therefore put aside (*the life where you formerly were disposed to*) all labor and trouble, and all deceit, and hypocrisies, and jealousies, backbiting and all sorts of slanderous speaking,

2 As newborn babes (*earnestly*) desire pure milk (*which is the reasoning and logic of God contained in the faith of Jesus Christ*), so that you may grow (*in wisdom and knowledge, and*) in union with Him thereby:

3 If indeed you have truly tasted that the Lord is (*good*) gracious (*and full of lovingkindness toward you*).

4 To whom coming, (*the Lord*), (*as*) a living stone, (*was*) rejected of men, but chosen of God and precious,

5 You also, as lively stones (*alive from the dead*), are built up (*upon Him*) a spiritual house, a holy priesthood, offering yourself (*a living sacrifice*) with spiritual sacrifices (*where the life you live in this world is only by God and His doing and not your own*), (*which sacrifice is*) acceptable to God through (*the faith revealed in*) Jesus Christ.

6 Therefore it is contained in scripture, (*thus says the Lord God*) behold I lay (*a stone*) in Zion (*for a foundation*) a chief cornerstone, chosen, precious: and he that believes upon Him will not ever be put to shame.

7 To you therefore who believe (*being fully persuaded of His lovingkindness toward you to give you His life*) He is precious: but to those who refuse to be persuaded, the stone which those who want to build (*their own house on their own*

foundation) rejected, this same (*stone*) has become the head of the corner,

8 And a stone that causes them to stumble at the truth and a rock which has become a snare to them who strike against (*and resist*) the word (*which God has spoken in Christ*), refusing to be persuaded (*of His lovingkindness to give them His life as a gift*): to which also those (*who are disobedient, refusing to be persuaded but*) continue in the way which has been judged beforehand as (*the way wherein they can only*) store up for themselves destruction (*being set against the way that leads to life*).

9 But you (*who are fully persuaded, believing that as His sons you*) are the favored offspring of God, a royal priesthood (*of kingly rank*), a holy nation (*set apart for Him to show you kindness for all the ages to come*), a peculiar people (*that are uniquely His own*); so that you would declare the goodness and lovingkindness of Him who has surnamed you His sons (*and led you*) out of darkness (*and death*) into His marvelous light (*and life*);

10 Which in time past were not a people but now (*has He gathered you unto Himself*) the people of God: which (*in times past*) had not received His mercy and grace (*for their affliction*), but now have received mercy and grace (*in Christ, being delivered from the affliction of death*).

11 My well beloved, I implore you as strangers in a strange land, that you keep yourselves (*abiding in His life, so that you might refrain from*) the lust for life in the world through the strength in your flesh (*and thereby disarm that*) which wars against (*and subverts*) the soul;

12 Having the manner of your life honorable among the (*unbelieving*) Gentiles: so, whereas they might (*have opportunity to*) speak against you as a troublemaker, instead, they witness your honest way of life, so that by seeing it God might be glorified in (*their hearts*) in the day of (*their own*) encounter with Him.

13 Submit yourselves to (*obey*) every (*established institution or*) ordinance of men who have authority over you for the

Lord's sake: whether it be to the ruler, as superior (*in matters of keeping order*);

14 Or to governors, treating them (*with respect for their authority*) as if they were sent by Him for the correction of those who act maliciously toward others, and for the praise of them that do well.

15 Because it is the will of God, that by doing that which is good you might (*glorify God*) silencing the accusations of foolish men, (*not in your own strength but*),

16 As (*one who is*) free (*and in bondage to no man*), and not using your freedom as an excuse to act venomously, but as one who (*finds the strength for their life in*) willingly allowing themselves to be served by God.

17 Honor all men (*as equal*). Love (*preferring the lives of*) the brotherhood of men (*especially those who you fellowship with in the faith*). Stand in awe of God. Honor your rulers.

18 As servants to those in authority be subject to them, giving all reverence; not only to the good and kind ones but also to the fraudulent and unjust.

19 Because in this is (*the*) grace (*of God*) that influences a man's heart, that if he be more conscious of the (*incorruptible*) life of God (*which he possesses*), which life cannot ever be hurt or injured by the (*death and*) injustices in the world, (*he would patiently endure*) even when he suffers grief and (*is treated*) unjustly.

20 Because what glory is there (*in the life*), (*where*) if, when you are harshly treated for your faults, you take it patiently? but (*rather, know*) that if, when you do good and suffer for it, you take it patiently, this is the life that God (*desires to freely serve you with*).

21 And even unto this (*incorruptible*) life (*that we see in Christ*) are you called: because Christ also suffered (*death and injustice*) for us, (*authoring*) for us the faith (*which He had toward the Father*), so that you (*being persuaded by the certainty of the same*) would be led in His footsteps:

1 Peter 3

22 (*Christ*) who did absolutely nothing (*in His own strength*) to preserve His life, neither was there any deceit found in His mouth:

23 (*Christ*) who, when He was railed against, did not rail back in return; when He unjustly suffered (*abuse and*) threats, He (*abused and*) threatened no one; but (*being fully persuaded that the Father was the good Shepherd and Bishop of His life*) He entrusted the care for Himself (*into the hands of*) Him who (*promised to preserve His life eternally and*) judges justly, (*and who has now put His justice for all men on full display in raising Christ from the dead in a glorified human body and seating Him at His right hand forever*):

24 (*Christ*) who (*offered*) Himself up for us (*for the conquering of*) our death (*to release us from the bondage of*) death by bearing it in His own body on the tree, so that we would see that being dead to death, (*we die no more*) but that (*resting in the Father*) we should live (*as He lives in immortal flesh and bone*) forever (*in the same life and immortality*): by whose stripes you were healed (*from the sting of death*).

25 Because you were as sheep going astray (*laboring in vain to preserve your own life*); but now you have been (*rescued from death*) brought back to the (*good*) Shepherd and Bishop of your life (*where you can find rest and peace in His life and pasture forever*).

Chapter 3

1 In the same way, wives, submit yourselves to your own husbands (*as one in union with you, as you are with the Lord*); so that even if any refuse to be persuaded by the word (*we preach*), they also might gain (*Christ*) by seeing how (*the fruit of God's*) life in their wives comes alongside the word (*preached*);

2 While they behold the pure innocence of your life (*in Christ*) along with your honor and respect for them (*as one in union with you, as you are with the Lord*).

3 Whose word is not made more beautiful by outward ornament like the braiding of your hair and wearing fine gold jewelry, or by putting on attractive clothing;

4 But through the inner man of that which (*flows from*) the heart, and which is (*born of God*) imperishable, even the (*inner*) ornament of a meek and peaceable spirit (*that rests in God and His strength to bring forth His life*), which is (*the one thing that*) in light of the desire of God's heart (*from the beginning to give you His life*) is so very precious to Him.

5 Because after this same way (*of inward adorning*) did the holy women of old, whose hope was (*also*) in God (*to fulfill His promise of life*), did adorning themselves, being subject to their own husbands:

6 Even like Sara who listened diligently to Abraham, calling him lord: whose children you are, (*seeing that you*) do well (*having the same spirit of faith toward God, not staggering in unbelief at His promise to give them His life as an inheritance*) wherein you also live (*a quiet and peaceful life*), without fear of any sudden terror.

7 Likewise, you husbands, live in union with your wives according to (*the*) knowledge (*of your union with Christ*), giving honor to the wife as (*precious*) the more delicate vessel, (*coming alongside her*) as being joint-heirs together of (*the same*) grace and kindness (*born*) from the life of God (*revealed in*) in Jesus Christ; so that your prayers (*might be one*) and not hindered (*by disagreement*).

8 Finally, may you all be of a single mind (*in Christ*), (*where you will*) find compassion (*and understanding*) for one another, loving each other as brothers, tenderhearted and humble (*in depending upon the Lord*):

9 (*To serve you with the life where you*) do not return evil for evil or railing for railing: but rather (*like Christ*) you return blessing; (*because*) knowing that you, yourself have been surnamed His son and that you will also inherit (*the*) blessing (*of His incorruptible life*).

10 Because the one that loves and desires (*the*) life (*that only He can give, esteeming it above all*), and longing to see good

days, (*will find it is His life that*) allows him to refrain his tongue from evil, and keep his lips from speaking deceit:

11 Allowing him to turn away from (*evil*) wherein you tried to establish your own life, (*rather*) to do good (*in allowing God to serve you with His life*); (*the life*) that allows him to find the peace (*that his heart*) has always longed for (*in Him*) and be overtaken in the rest that it brings to him.

12 Because the eyes (*and the mind*) of the Lord are (*always*) on (*His children*) to give them His life, and His ears are open to the cries of their hearts: but the face of the Lord is against (*the way that brings destruction*) in them that do evil (*by rejecting His gift of life for the way that can only serve them with destruction and death*).

13 And who is he that can bring harm to you, if (*the life*) you eagerly desire (*is the incorruptible life that He gives*) which is good?

14 But and (*even*) if you suffer (*an unjust punishment in the flesh*) for doing well, you (*remain*) happy (*in this blessed life, knowing that the life you possess cannot be hurt or injured*): and (*being fully persuaded of that life*) you are not afraid of the terror (*that men can bring*), neither are you troubled;

15 But (*just as you know you are set apart in God's heart so also*) set apart Christ (*the word of eternal life about you*) as Lord in your hearts: and always be ready to give an answer to every man that asks you for an account concerning the (*sure*) hope that is in you (*of the same life in Christ*) with gentleness and reverence:

16 Having a good conscience (*which is one that rests in God and His ability to establish His life in you*), so that, should they speak against you (*and your way of life, trusting in the Lord*), they may see (*that it is their hope to establish their own life which disappoints*) and not your hope in Christ of which they have falsely accused you.

17 Because if the hope and desire of God be (*that you inherit His incorruptible life*), it is better that when you suffer persecution under the injustice of death that you do well, in placing your hope in God (*who promised you His life*) and not

in yourself which is evil (*and that which causes you to labor in vain*).

18 Because Christ (*our high priest*) has also suffered under the (*same*) injustice of death for (*the purpose of*) sending death away from us, the just (*whose flesh rested in the sure hope of the Father to protect and persevere His life*) on behalf of the unjust (*who had all their lifetime suffered under the injustice of death laboring in vain in their flesh*), so that He might bring us to God (*our Father, where we also would rest in Him*), (*by the testimony of Jesus Christ, who*) being put to death in the flesh, was made alive (*in immortal flesh and bone*) by the Spirit (*of God*).

19 By the same (*Spirit*) which He also (*came, declaring the gospel in Noah*) to those souls (*who were suffering*) in bondage (*and laboring under the reign of death*);

20 Who at that time refused to be persuaded (*that God's desire was to save their lives from destruction and to preserve it in Him*), (*during the time*) when the patience of God waited (*120 years*) in the days of Noah, while the ark was being prepared, the ark (*being a figure of Christ*), in which, a few, that is eight souls were saved (*from the world filled with labor and anguish that perished, being overflowed*) by water (*which also carried them to safety being pitched within and without in the ark*).

21 The same (*is a*) figure of (*the*) baptism (*into Christ's death and resurrection, that being buried with Christ in His death, so are we also pitched within and without and pass from death unto life*) which (*baptism*) does also now save us, not by the washing away of the filth of the flesh (*which could never purge our conscience from death*), but the answer of a good conscience toward God (*that has freed us from death and the fear of death, where our sure hope is in God and His promise of eternal life*), by the resurrection of Jesus Christ:

22 Who is gone into heaven and is (*seated*) on the right hand of God; the angels and (*all*) authorities and powers being made subject to Him.

Chapter 4

1 Therefore seeing as Christ has suffered for us (*being put to death*) in the flesh, arm yourselves likewise with the same mind: because he who has suffered (*being put to death*) in the flesh (*dies no more and being dead to death*) has ceased from enlisting his members to preserve his own life;

2 So that he would no longer live the rest of his days in the flesh (*in bondage*) to (*bring forth*) the desires of men (*for life, through the strength contained in his flesh, which only served him with death*), but rather by the faith of the Son of God (*which serves with life everlasting*).

3 Because we have already spent enough days (*in the flesh*) where we carried out the same way of life as the Gentiles (*as if we also were alienated from the promises, having no hope and without God*) when we walked in sensuality, lust, drunkenness, debauchery, carousing and the unjust worship of false gods (*and every other thing that could never serve us with life*).

4 And those (*who do such things are confused by and*) think it strange that you do not take part (*with them*) in the same excessive debauchery, which is why they speak against you:

5 Who (*themselves*) will judge (*the word in their own heart whether it be*) against Him who has already judged (*which word brings life to both*) the living and the dead.

6 For to this end was the gospel proclaimed (*through the Spirit of Christ*) even to (*those who are now*) dead (*having never received the promises*), so that they might be judged (*in the same manner*) as (*us*) men in the flesh (*who have been preached the gospel through Holy Ghost sent down from heaven*), that all (*who live*) might live according to (*the Spirit of*) God in their heart.

7 But the end of all things (*that are not eternal*) has drawn near to you, (*your salvation is closer now than when you first believed*): let therefore Christ regulate your thoughts and your mind as you watch and pray.

8 And above all things (*that you might*) have constant union with (*His*) passionate love among yourselves (*and one for another*): because (*His*) love (*abiding in you*) will cover a great number of offenses.

9 (*For abiding in His love you will find*) generosity (*born in you*) toward guests and strangers, (*showing kindness*) one for another (*without obligation*) or complaining.

10 Just like every man (*who*) has (*freely*) received the gift (*of eternal life*) even so (*be you*) ministers of the same life one to another, as good stewards of the many unique and precious intricacies of the grace of God (*given each one of us in Christ Jesus*).

11 If any man (*desires*) to speak (*the truth revealed in Christ*), let him speak as (*one declaring*) the very words and utterances (*that come*) from God; if any man (*be a*) minister (*of Christ*), let him do it (*in humility, seeing that it is through the gifts and*) the ability which God has given him (*and not his own ability that men will experience God's life in the midst of tribulation*): so that God in all (*these*) things might be exalted (*as the One who brings forth the fruit of His life in us*) through Jesus Christ, whose name (*being spoken well of and*) glorified (*in men's heart, will they call upon in the day of affliction*) seeing that He has dominion (*over the death and corruption in the world*) forever and ever. Amen.

12 Beloved, do not be (*shocked or*) surprised concerning the fiery ordeal which will come to try you (*seeing as we live in a world presently filled with death and corruption*), as if some unique thing is happening to (*only*) you:

13 But joy (*comes in being fully persuaded that*) just as you have shared in the sufferings of Christ (*under the injustice of death in the world*) that you may also rejoice with exceedingly great joy (*in knowing the certainty of sharing in the same glory that was*) revealed in Him.

14 If you are mocked (*and persecuted*) for (*believing on*) the name of Christ (*as your own inheritance*), you are happy because (*you know that*) the Spirit of glory and of God rests upon you (*with the power of an indestructible life*): on the part

of (*those who mock*) is He (*devalued and*) spoken maliciously of, but in your heart is He (*precious*), esteemed and glorified.

15 But let none of you (*who name the name of Christ*) suffer as a murderer, or a thief, or as a malcontent, or as one who meddles in other men's affairs.

16 However if (*any man suffers injustice*) as a follower of Christ, let him not be ashamed (*for Christ also suffered injustice*); but let him (*like Christ*) glorify God (*as the One who judges justly in preserving his life eternally*) in the same inheritance of Christ.

17 Because now is the time when the judgment (*that was from the beginning*) has begun in us (*who rest in God for the same life and justice revealed in the resurrection of Jesus Christ*); (*to shine as a light in the darkness*) in us who are the house of God: and since (*the judgment that allows us to rest in God to bring forth His life free from our works*) has first appeared in us, what will be the end of those who refuse to be persuaded to rest (*in God to freely give them His life, that was revealed*) in the gospel of God (*seeing as they reject that judgment unto life*)?

18 And if (*we think*) that the righteous (*are only*) saved through great struggle (*from the suffering in the world*), where would the ungodly and those laboring to preserve their own lives (*ever find the strength to overcome the death and corruption in the world*), so that they might also appear (*in the light of His life*)?

19 Therefore let them that suffer (*persecution and injustice, suffer as Christ did*) according to the will of God (*resting in the certainty of His promise to protect and preserve their life in Christ*) and (*who being fully persuaded will*) do well in committing the keeping of their lives to Him as unto a faithful Creator.

Chapter 5

1 Therefore, do I exhort the elders among you, being an elder myself as well as an eyewitness of the sufferings (*and the*

resurrection) of Christ, and a sharer in the glory that will be revealed:

2 Shepherd the flock of God that is among you (*with this word of eternal life*), looking diligently to their care, not by obligation, but of your own accord, and not for dishonest or personal gain but eagerly from your passion (*for the Lord and the love of God for all people*) that is in you.

3 Neither as one who exercises power and control over others (*who are co-sharers with you in God's inheritance*) but as examples who walk alongside them.

4 And when the chief Shepherd, (*our Lord Jesus*) is revealed (*from heaven*), you (*all*) will receive a victory crown of glory that will never fade away.

5 Likewise, you younger (*ministers of Christ*), submit yourselves to the elder. Yes, (*so that*) all of you would be subject one to another (*as members of one body*) and be clothed with humility (*which brings glory to God*): because God (*in His great love for us*) has set Himself against the (*way of*) the proud (*to exalt themselves unto life by their own strength and perish in death*) and gives grace (*to freely experience His life*) to the humble (*who are persuaded that the sufficiency and strength for their life is only found resting in and allowing Him to freely serve them with it*).

6 Humble yourselves therefore (*to be served by*) the mighty (*and loving*) hand of God (*resting in His strength alone as the sufficiency for you to experience His life*), so that He might (*be the one to*) exalt you (*at every fitting opportunity*) and in due time:

7 Casting all the care (*and responsibility for your life*) upon Him; for He cares for you (*like no other can, to preserve your life in Him now and forever*).

8 Be of a sound mind and watchful, for your adversary comes to accuse your heart (*with thoughts that originate from*) the devil (*whose wisdom has been planted in the world*) and as a roaring lion (*which makes a lot of noise*) is always looking for an opportunity to swallow up, (*overwhelming*) whoever will allow it:

1 Peter 5

9 Whose accusation (*you*) withstand (*by resting*) in the faith (*of Jesus Christ, who already stood in the face of it for you*), knowing that the same suffering and afflictions that (*were in Him*) and in your brothers are in the world.

10 But the God of all grace (*and mercy*), who has called us to His eternal glory (*which He purposed and promised from the beginning*) and has now through Christ Jesus, (*fulfilled the promise and given us this sure hope*) that after you have suffered a short while (*in the world*), (*He will*) make you perfect, establish, strengthen, and settle you (*in His life and immortality forever*).

11 To Him be all glory and dominion forever and ever (*throughout all the ages, world without end*). Amen.

12 I am sending this short letter by Sil-va'nus, who I hear is a faithful brother to you, where I have written briefly, exhorting, and testifying that this is the true grace of God wherein you stand.

13 The church that is at Bab'y-lon, and all the fellow sharers (*of His life*) together with you, salutes you; as does Mar'cus my son (*in the faith*).

14 Greet one another with a kiss of love. Peace be with you all that are in Christ Jesus. Amen.

The Second Epistle of
PETER
The Faith Translation

Chapter 1

1 Simon Peter, a bondservant (*who willingly belongs to*) and is an apostle of Jesus Christ, to those that (*share with us in His life*) having obtained an equally precious faith through (*the revelation of*) the justice of God (*to give us His blessing and life as a gift*) and (*who has served us with that life through*) our Savior Jesus Christ:

2 (*His*) grace and peace are multiplied to you through the knowledge of God revealed in Jesus Christ our Lord (*to whom belongs all the treasures of wisdom and knowledge*),

3 (*Who has*) accordingly through His own divine power and ability given to us all things that pertain to (*us experiencing the substance of His*) life and Godlikeness, (*which comes*) through the knowledge of Him (*revealed in the faith of Jesus Christ*) in which He has called us (*through the spirit of faith*) to (*the same*) glory and virtue:

4 And through (*this faith*) is given to us (*the sure hope of these*) magnificent and precious promises (*surpassing all that we could ask or think*): so that by these you might share in the life and nature of God and having (*your flesh put to rest by His life*) you will escape the corruption that is contained in the world from (*the*) lust (*to bring forth life by your flesh*).

5 And for this reason, give all diligence (*to hearken*) to this faith (*which lavishly supplies*) you with (*His goodness and*) virtue, and (*along with*) virtue knowledge;

6 And (*along with*) knowledge self-control; and (*along with*) self-control patience; and (*along with*) patience Godlikeness.

7 And (*along with*) Godlikeness brotherly kindness and (*along with*) brotherly kindness love.

8 Because if these things (*which are contained in the faith of Jesus Christ*) be (*born*) in you (*by hearkening to this faith*), and (*abide and*) abound (*in your heart*), they (*will*) make you so that you will not be barren or unfruitful in the knowledge of our Lord Jesus Christ.

9 But the one who lacks these things is blind (*not hearkening diligently to the faith revealed in Jesus Christ*), and (*therefore*)

cannot see very far off, and has (*quickly*) forgotten that he was purged from (*the bondage of*) death wherein he formerly labored in vain for life.

10 Therefore brethren, give all diligence (*to listen closely and keep hearing*) the faith (*of Jesus Christ*) to make your calling unto the life that He has chosen you for (*from the beginning*) a certainty (*in your heart*): because if you do this (*one thing*) you will (*in no way*) ever fall:

11 Because in this (*faith*) has (*He has given to you*) the way that keeps you and has served you abundantly with His life, unto the everlasting kingdom of our Lord and Savior Jesus Christ.

12 Therefore, I will always be ready (*and constantly*) remind you of all these things, even though you (*might already*) know them, (*lest you forget*) and (*so that you would*) be established (*and strengthened*) by this present truth (*abiding in you*).

13 Yes, I esteem (*this faith as the thing that will form His life in us*) so that as long as I am in this body, I will stir you up (*constantly*) by putting you in remembrance;

14 Knowing that shortly I must put off this body, indeed as the Lord Jesus has shown me.

15 Now therefore I will be diligent (*with the faith*) so that after I am gone, you might (*always*) have these things in your remembrance.

16 For we have not followed (*after nor are we repeating someone else's*) cleverly devised tales, when we made known to you the power and coming of our Lord Jesus Christ but were eyewitnesses of His (*glory and*) majesty.

17 For He received from God the Father, honor, and glory, when (*we heard with our own ears*) a voice that came and spoke to Him from (*out of the clouds*) full of (*glory and*) majesty saying, this is My beloved Son in whom I am well pleased.

18 And this voice that came from heaven we heard when we were with Him in the holy mountain.

19 We also have a more sure word of prophecy (*contained in the faith of Jesus Christ that came out of the grave in immortal flesh*); wherein it would do you all well that you take heed (*and*

hearken diligently to), as you would to a light that shines in a dark place (*for He is the light unto our feet and the lamp unto our way*), (*He shines*) until the day dawn, and the day star arise in your hearts:

20 Knowing this first, that there is no prophecy of the scripture that is of any private interpretation (*but all are speaking about Christ, the word that has been now made immortal flesh, He is the full counsel of God*).

21 Because the prophecy that came in times past (*through the law and the prophets*), came not by the will of man: but through men who were ordained to speak the oracles of God, who spoke as they were moved by the Holy Ghost (*the things concerning Christ, the word now made immortal flesh in the resurrection*).

Chapter 2

1 However, there were false prophets also among the people (*in those days*), just as there will be false teachers among you (*today*), who will deceitfully bring in destructive and erroneous doctrines (*outside of Christ, the word made immortal flesh and filled with their own private interpretations*), denying indeed the Lord that bought them, and (*who*) bring on themselves swift destruction.

2 And many will follow after their (*deceitful and*) destructive ways, through whom the way of the truth will be maligned (*and spoken disparagingly*).

3 And through their greedy desire for gain (*and unbridled lust for life through the strength contained in their flesh*) will they with carefully crafted words (*that suit their own vain imaginations*) make merchandise of you (*for their own personal gain*): who even now (*bring*) judgment (*upon themselves, seeing they have set themselves against the judgment of God unto life*), and (*having a heart contrary to that judgment, their own hearts are actively*) condemning them to destruction.

4 Because if (*the judgment of*) God (*against death and its corrupt wisdom*) did not spare the angels that left their original

design (*to be messengers of the way that leads men to destruction*), but cast them out from heaven, delivering them into the pits of darkness, to be kept unto (*the day of*) judgment;

5 And spared not the old world (*filled with labor and anguish*) but saved Noah and eight other persons (*from it*), (*Noah being*) a preacher of the everlasting kindness of God toward men to preserve their lives, (*saving them by*) bringing in the flood upon the world (*that was serving men with death*) and (*where*) those who considered themselves unworthy, (*rejected*) God's judgment to preserve their lives, perished (*in the flood*).

6 And (*similarly by*) turning the cities of Sodom and Gomorrah into ashes, has He judged and purposed to destroy all that which brings suffering and is against men's lives, setting (*this as*) an example to those that should afterward disregard the (*incorruptible*) life that God (*freely*) gives in exchange for the (*corruptible*) life (*they can give themselves*) that perishes in death;

7 But (*He*) delivered Lot who was just (*in revering and trusting God to preserve his life*), (*despite being continually*) distressed by and exposed to their unrestrained lust for life through their (*sensually*), being animated by every desire contained in their flesh (*to do many things which are vile and*) wicked, (*He rescued and preserved his life*):

8 Because (*even being a*) just man (*who trusted and revered God*) was he tormented in his mind and emotions, being among them, seeing and hearing from day to day the deeds of those who transgress God's way unto life (*for their own way*);

9 The Lord knows (*the heart of*) those who place their trust in Him, to deliver them (*from*) out of affliction (*and death*), and (*is longsuffering*) to reserve (*His judgment against the way that perishes in death*) in those who refuse to be persuaded, until the day of judgment (*seeing as they store up for themselves the same end*):

10 Especially (*the way of the serpent*) in those who walk in their own lust (*for life through the strength contained in their flesh*), who defile themselves and despise authority. They are

blatantly self-willed and are not afraid (*but quick*) to speak slanderously against those (*who God has deemed as valuable and*) are worthy of His good opinion.

11 Whereas (*even the*) angels, who are (*presently*) greater in strength and power (*than them*), dare not to bring a harsh accusation against them before the Lord.

12 But these (*men*), have been (*marked by the beast*) and are like wild beasts (*who lack any rational thought*) but are made for capture and destruction, who speak insultingly of things that they do not even understand; and will utterly perish in their own corruption (*and destruction which they have stored up for themselves*);

13 And (*they*) will receive the reward (*which the*) injustice (*of exchanging the incorruptible life which God freely gives for the corruptible life they can give themselves pays with*), as they currently think it satisfying (*to their flesh*) to openly live in excess and from every sensual desire, they are (*like*) spots and blemishes (*on a pure garment*) who take delight in their own deception, even while they eat together with you;

14 Having eyes (*filled*) full of (*spiritual*) adultery (*which is idolatry, where they are always looking to anything but God to serve them with a good life in the world*), and (*because they can never find satisfaction or rest in anything but God*) they cannot ever cease from lusting after the corruptible life they can serve themselves with through their flesh; enticing the souls of those who are not yet established (*in Christ*): with a heart (*filled with what they can gather to themselves*) have they exercised it in lustful ways; (*whereby they make themselves like*) children who are still under the curse of death (*seeing as they continue in that cursed life*):

15 Which have forsaken the right way (*unto life*) and have gone out of the way (*that brings life, peace, and rest*), following after the way of Ba'laam the son of Bo'sor (*and his greedy desire for gain*), who loved the wages of that cursed life (*that perishes more than the gift of God's incorruptible life*);

16 But (*who*) was rebuked for the iniquity in his heart (*which was a heart persuasion that disregarded God's blessing and*

life as a gift): and who was spoken to by a donkey in a man's voice (*correcting and*) forbidding the insanity of the prophet.

17 These (*men*) are (*like empty*) wells without water, (*and unstable*) clouds that are tossed by the wind (*without rest*); to whom (*heap to themselves destruction and*) the certainty of the blackness of darkness forever.

18 For when they speak their arrogant (*but*) worthless words (*void of any power to quicken one to life*), they entice (*other men's*) desire for life through the strength contained in their flesh, (*appealing to*) their excessive sensual desires, and these men who having previously (*seen there was freedom in Christ*), fled from, escaping (*the corruption in the world*) and those who were living in (*this*) error (*that leads to destruction*).

19 While they promise them freedom, they themselves are (*still*) slaves to (*the*) corruption (*and death in the world*): because whatever a man is overcome by, the same is he brought in bondage.

20 Because if after they have escaped the corruption in the world (*that caused them to labor for life through the strength contained in their flesh*) through the knowledge that the Lord and Savior Jesus Christ (*has conquered their death in the flesh in the resurrection*), their hearts become entangled again, laboring to be free from the death in the world through the strength of their flesh (*and not Christ*) and are thereby overcome, the latter end is worse than the beginning (*seeing there is no other name by which there is salvation to overcome death*).

21 For it would have been better for them to be ignorant of the way to inherit God's life, than to have known the goodness of God to give them blessing and life as a gift and turn (*away*) from that holy commandment (*He*) delivered to them (*in Jesus Christ*).

22 But the thing that happens to them is according to the truth contained in the proverb which says, the dog is turned again to his own vomit (*having tasted of the goodness of God to give them His incorruptible life as a gift they return again to eat of the corruptible life they can serve themselves with*); and

(*like*) the sow that (*after she*) was washed went wallowing (*again*) in the mud.

Chapter 3

1 Beloved, this is the second letter that I have written to you and in both I have endeavored to stir up your pure minds by putting you in remembrance (*of the holy commandment, eternal life, that is contained in the faith of our Lord Jesus Christ*):

2 So that you would be mindful of that (*when you read*) the words which were spoken beforehand by the holy prophets and (*now*) by us who are the apostles (*and messengers*) of the Lord and Savior Jesus Christ:

3 Knowing this first, that in the last days (*of death in the earth*) there will come scoffers, who scoff (*being willingly ignorant of God's desire*) and walking according to their own lust,

4 And saying, where is the promise of His coming? For since the time the fathers have fallen asleep, all things continue as they were from the beginning of creation.

5 For in (*saying*) this they have determined to ignore (*the truth*) that the heavens which did exist long ago by the word of God, and the earth that stood out from the water and divided from the waters (*did by the same word of God*):

6 Whereby we also know that the world that was at that time, perished, being overflowed with water:

7 But the heavens and the earth, which are now, by the same word (*of God*) are kept (*along with the works which men have treasured up*), reserved for fire (*to be tried as to what sort they are*) against (*the testimony which God gave in His Son that has already been proven by fire*) for the day of judgment and (*the day of*) the destruction of men who having rejected God's life will perish (*seeing they exchange the testimony of His life for their own*).

8 However beloved, do not be ignorant of this one thing, that one day with the Lord is like a thousand years, and a thousand years is like one day.

9 The Lord is not (*neglectful or*) slow concerning His promise (*to come in the fire of His life and to destroy and remove every remnant of death from the earth*), as some men count slowness; but (*in His*) long-suffering toward us (*has He appointed a day and time*), (*because*) He is not willing (*and finds no pleasure*) that anyone should perish (*in the death that laboring to preserve their lives in their own strength will serve them with*), but that all men would be persuaded of the life (*they see in Christ Jesus*) which He has promised to serve them with, (*relying upon His strength and ability alone to protect and preserve their lives eternally*).

10 But (*of a certainty*) the day of the Lord will come like a thief (*who sneaks*) in the night (*at an hour you think not*); in the which the heavens will pass away with a great noise, and the elements (*of this world*) will melt with fervent heat, the earth also and the (*corruptible*) works that are (*contained*) therein will be burned up (*when He comes to baptize in the fire of His life*).

11 Seeing as all these (*corruptible*) things will be dissolved (*and completely done away with*), what quality (*and testimony*) of life should you partake in (*to be as you ought to be*) in the (*incorruptible*) life and Godlikeness you were set apart for,

12 Where you with hopeful expectation earnestly desire the coming of the day of God, in which the fire (*of His life*) from heaven will be released and all the (*corruptible*) elements (*in the world*) will melt with fervent heat?

13 Nevertheless, we (*who are born of the Spirit*), according to His promise (*of eternal life*), look for new heavens and a new earth, (*where there is no longer any remnant of corruption and death and*) wherein only the life and immortality of God dwells.

14 Therefore, beloved, seeing as you look (*desiring*) for such things, be diligent (*with the faith*) so that you may be found of Him in peace (*resting in His promise of life*), (*bearing the testimony that God gave of you in the Son which is*) without spot, and blameless.

2 Peter 2

15 And consider that the patience (*and long-suffering*) of our Lord is (*the goodness of God that leads men to repentance unto*) salvation (*from death and destruction*); just as our beloved brother Paul has (*also explained*) and written to you about, according to the wisdom given to him (*by the Lord Jesus*);

16 Just as he also has done in all his letters, speaking about these things (*concerning the grace of our Lord Jesus Christ from the law and the prophets*); in which some things are difficult to understand (*outside of the faith and the wisdom of our Lord Jesus*), which they that are ignorant and unestablished distort, as they do with all the scriptures to their own destruction.

17 You therefore, beloved, knowing these things beforehand, take heed (*to be diligent with the faith, to hear and keep on hearing*) lest you are also and are led away with the (*same*) error of those who are filled with labors and annoyances, and from your heart's reliance upon Him.

18 But (*as you hear and keep on hearing how God has conquered your death and freely given you the same life you behold in Jesus Christ, will you*) grow in grace and in the knowledge of our Lord and Savior Jesus Christ. To Him be all glory, both now (*in this present world*) and forever. Amen.

The First Epistle of

JOHN

The Faith Translation

Chapter 1

1 That which was, which is, and will forever be God, the Word of eternal life that was with God in the beginning when He hovered over the face of the deep and said "let there be light", the same light and life which He promised and that has come out of the grave immortal, the light and the life of all men, which we have heard with our own ears and beheld His glory with our own eyes, and our hands have handled, that which came forth from the abundance of the Father's heart, the Word of life made immortal flesh.

2 For the life that was manifest from the grave in immortal flesh and bone, we have seen it and do bear witness to it, and would like to make known to you, giving shape and form to it, declaring unto you that the eternal life which was with the Father from the beginning was manifested unto us not as a spirit but in immortal human flesh.

3 That life which we have seen and heard, do we declare unto you so that you can have fellowship with and share in the eternal life that is in the Father and His Son Jesus Christ.

4 And these things I write unto you so that you may know Him and be certain you have eternal life, that your joy might be full and complete in Him.

5 This then is the message which we have heard of Him, and declare unto you, that God, the only immortal, is only light and life, and in Him is no death or darkness at all.

6 If we say that we have fellowship with Him in Whom there is only light and life, and with His incorruptible life and we walk as if we are still in death and darkness, laboring to build and preserve our own life in the world, we lie, and do not the truth that is in Him.

7 If we walk in the light and life that God has promised from the beginning and was made immortal flesh in the resurrection, in His eternal life that cannot ever be hurt or injured by the death and corruption in the world; knowing that as He is only light and life; and has freely given us that same life which is the light of all men, so also are we in the light having true fellowship in that life one with another, and

the blood that ran out of His Son Jesus Christ allows our flesh to go to rest; purging our hearts and minds from all the labor and toil of building our own lives, to serve and be served by the living God.

8 If we say we could partake of that life apart from our death being conquered in the flesh, we deceive ourselves and the truth is not in us.

9 If we agree with Him that our death needed to be conquered in the flesh; we also see that He has spoken a word to us in His Son; persuading our hearts of His justice in removing our death from us, cleansing our conscience, and divorcing us from all the injustice that death has brought us.

10 If we say that death was not the thing reigning over us and causing us to preserve our own lives through the strength contained in our flesh, we make Him a liar, and His word is not in us.

Chapter 2

1 My little children, these things I write unto you that you might rest in Him and His life, so that you do not enlist your members to clothe yourself with the life in the world that perishes in death but find rest in the certainty of Him clothing you in His incorruptible life. And if any man finds himself pressed in by the death and corruption in the world telling him that he lacks life, we have One who is with the Father, and who testifies to our hearts of the certainty of our life, Jesus Christ the righteous and firstborn from the dead.

2 And in Him has God shown Himself favorable toward us in removing our death: and not ours only but the entire world.

3 And here is how we know that we have become intimately acquainted with Him, when we believe that He is the word of eternal life that was promised from the beginning and made immortal flesh in the resurrection, the Spirit of truth is born in us and keeps us.

4 He that says, I know Him, but denies the One who is the Word of eternal life that was from the beginning and that came

out of the grave in immortal flesh, is a liar and the truth is not in him.

5 But whosoever hears and is kept by His Spirit, abiding in this Word of eternal life, in him truly is the hope of God to love and be good to him for the ages to come made perfect in him: And by abiding in this word, we allow Him to serve us with that life, knowing we are in Him.

6 He that says he abides in Him, abides in the Word of eternal life, and ought to walk even as He walked, knowing that as He possesses a life that cannot be hurt or injured by the corruption in the world, so also do we have the certainty of the same life to be revealed in us.

7 Brethren, I write no new teaching unto you but rather that same truth contained in the Word of eternal life which you have heard and was with the Father from the beginning. The truth you have heard of old wherein God gave His command, "let there be light", the Word of life, is the same Word of eternal life that was from the beginning which has now been made immortal flesh.

8 So again, I write a new commandment unto you of the Word of life made immortal flesh which contains the thing that is true in Him and you: Because it declares that in Him death was abolished, and the darkness has passed, and the true light of the life and immortality promised from the beginning now shines upon us in the face of Jesus Christ.

9 He that says he is in light and hates his brother is in darkness and does not see how his death has been conquered in the flesh.

10 He that loves his brother abides in the light, where he finds his life born from the Word of eternal life, a life that cannot ever be hurt or injured by the death and corruption in the world, but he rests in the life where he does not need to work to preserve himself and in that life, there is no occasion of stumbling in him.

11 But the one who hates his brother is in darkness, walking out of the way, and does not know where he is going, and not seeing that his death has been conquered in the flesh, he is

animated by death to preserve his own life in the flesh, because the death contained in his body has blinded his eyes.
12 I write to you, little children, because you know your death has been sent away from you because the Father who promised you His life from the beginning has manifested His life in immortal flesh in the Son.
13 I write to you, fathers because you have known Him that is from the beginning. I write to you, young men because in Him, you find your strength to overcome the word that the wicked one has planted in the world. I write to you, little children because you have come to know Him as Father.
14 I have written to you, fathers, because you have long known Him and His word from the beginning, I have written to you, young men, because you find your strength in the word of eternal life that is abiding in you, whereby you have overcome the death and corruption in the world.
15 Love not the life that is in the world that perishes in death, neither the corruptible things that you can gather to yourself in the world. If any man esteems the life the world offers and can serve him with over the Father's life, he has never truly known the love of the Father which can only be born in his heart from abiding in the Word of life which He has spoken in the Son wherein He promised to preserve his life in Him eternally.
16 For all that the world can offer and produce is death; for the things in the world are these: the lust for life that can be born in your flesh from the death and corruption in the world, the lust of your eyes seeing that the way that brings death looks good for food to make one wise, gathering a good life to oneself and the pride of boasting in what you can do, to gather or to possess a good life through the strength contained in your own hand, none of these come from the Father but are of the death in the world.
17 And the world passes away, along with the lust that death brought: but he who trusts in the Word of life that God has spoken about Him in Christ abides with Him in the same life forever.

1 John 2

18 Little children, it is death's last days: and as you have heard that those who oppose Christ shall come, even now are there many in the world who oppose Christ; and by this, we know that it is death's last days in the earth.

19 They went out from us to serve other gods, for if they had been abiding in the same fellowship as us, they would have no doubt continued with us: but they went out of the way so that it might be manifest that they were not all of us in the truth.

20 But you have an inward persuasion that comes from the Holy One, and by Him do you know all truth.

21 I have not written unto you because you do not know the truth, but because you know Him who is the truth, and by Him can discern the lie, knowing that no lie is born of the truth found in Him.

22 Who is a liar but he that denies that Jesus is the Christ; the Word of eternal life made immortal flesh? He is against Christ, that denies the Father was in the Son.

23 Whosoever denies the Son does not abide in the truth and the same has denied the Father who is in Him: but he that confesses that Jesus is the Son of God has confessed the Father also and has both the Father and the Son abiding in him.

24 Allow, therefore, the Word of eternal life which you have heard from the beginning and that came forth from the heart of the Father, being made immortal flesh in the Son, to abide in you. For if that Word of eternal life which you have heard from the beginning remains in you, so also does it keep you in fellowship and in union with the Son, and the Father.

25 And this is the promise which He has promised us from the beginning and has come out of the grave in immortal flesh in the resurrection, eternal life.

26 These things have I written to you concerning anyone who would come to seduce you with a word that is contrary to the truth found in Him.

27 But the Spirit of life which He promised, and you have received of Him will abide and remain in you so that you do

not need anyone to teach you: and the same Spirit that teaches you all things pertaining to the truth, and discerns the lie, so also will guide you so that you abide in Him.

28 And now, little children, abide in Him who is the Word that the Father has testified about us; so that, when He shall appear, we may have confidence, and not be ashamed to stand before Him at his coming.

29 If we know that the One who came from the heart of the Father to testify on our behalf regarding the promise of His life and immortality has been raised up in His incorruptible life, we know that everyone who trusts in Him and His promise of eternal life is born of Him unto the same life.

Chapter 3

1 Behold in the face of Jesus Christ the width, the length, the depth, and height of the love that the Father has bestowed upon us, that we should be surnamed by "I AM", the sons of God: therefore the world doesn't recognize us as sons because it never knew the One whom He sent.

2 Beloved, right now in this world we are the sons of God, possessing His life and fellowship, filled with the glory and honor from our Father, and though it has not yet manifest in our bodies what we shall be: we know with certainty, that when He appears in all His glory, we shall also, appear in His likeness; for we shall see ourselves in His face, as the beloved sons of God and as He is fashioned in His glorious body, so shall we be also.

3 And every man that has their hope settled in Him, in the certainty of the same life and immortality that came out of the grave in immortal flesh and bone rests in the only hope that can purify his own heart, even as He is pure; holy and undefiled by the death and corruption in the world.

4 Whosoever rejects Christ as the only Word that can serve us with eternal life, practices lawlessness, and transgresses the teaching and instruction of God unto life: for to reject Christ is the lawlessness that perishes in death.

1 John 3

5 And we know that He was manifested to send our death away; and in Him is no death or darkness at all.

6 Whosoever abides in Him, that serves us with His blessing and life as a gift, goes to rest, no longer working to establish his own life in the world which perishes in death: whosoever labors and toils to build his own life has not seen that He has conquered their death, neither known Him who has promised and desires to freely give him His blessing and life as a gift.

7 Little children, let no man deceive you, robbing you of this truth: he who believes that there is only One who is the true witness and testimony of his life has the certainty of the same life, and just as He is the possessor of an incorruptible life at the Father's right hand, even so, are you in the world.

8 He who goes about to establish and preserve his own life in the world through the strength contained in his flesh misses the mark of eternal life; forfeiting the life and immortality of God as his inheritance, perishing in death, being born from the corrupt wisdom of the serpent; who was a liar from the beginning, telling man that he would not die in trying to establish a life apart from God, but in fact, that life only ever served man with death. For this reason, the Son of God came as a man in dying flesh, refusing to establish or preserve His own life in the world, being put to death in the flesh but was quickened by the Spirit and has come out from the grave in immortal flesh and bone, destroying this wisdom along with the death it served us with.

9 Whosoever believes Jesus is the Christ is born of the Spirit of God and does not need to enlist their members to establish their own life but their flesh rests in the certainty of His blessing and life as a gift; and because His Spirit remains in them; death has no more dominion over them being dead to death and alive to God.

10 In this saying are those who are born of God, and those animated by the wisdom of the serpent manifest: whosoever does not rest in God and His promise to give him eternal life as a gift is not born of God, neither does he find love for his brother born in him.

11 For this is eternal life, the message that you have heard from the beginning, and was made immortal flesh in the resurrection of Jesus, it is God clothing you in the fruit of His life whereby you have love one for another.

12 Unlike Cain, who was born from the corrupt wisdom of that wicked one and slew his brother. And why did he slew him? Because his works to produce a good life were filled with labors and annoyances to gather fruit unto himself which brings forth hatred, backbiting and murder and his brother trusted in God to clothe him with the fruit of His life.

13 Knowing this, marvel not, my brethren, if the world hates you also.

14 Because we know that we have passed from death unto the life that cannot be hurt or injured by the death and corruption in the world, we love all the brethren. He that does not love his brother abides in darkness not knowing his death has been conquered.

15 Whosoever abides in darkness, under the influence of death, hates his brother and is a murderer like his father the devil: and you know that no one abiding in eternal life is a murderer.

16 Here is how we can have intimacy and experience the love of God, because He came as a man laying down His life for us: and has also freely given us the life where we prefer one another, laying down our life for the brethren.

17 But if someone has worldly possessions and sees his brother in need of such and closes off their true heart of compassion for him, how does that allow him to experience intimacy with the love of God?

18 My little children, let us not just talk about love, but abiding in Him let us find our hearts saturated in the truth so that we can experience the overflow of His love in us toward others.

19 And by abiding in Him we can have intimacy with the only truth that assures our hearts to stand before Him with confidence.

20 For even if our own heart condemns us, God's judgement of innocence is greater than our heart because He knows all things, so, abide in Him who is the only one who can discern our hearts for us.

21 Beloved, if our heart does not condemn us to a life where we think that He has commanded us to bring forth fruit, but rather know that it is His good pleasure to clothe us in the fruit of His life, then we will come boldly and stand before Him with confidence.

22 And we know that all that He has is ours, so that whatever we ask is received of Him, and because we have kept His commandment to abide in Him and His promise to clothe us in His light and life, which is the command that is pleasing in His sight.

23 And His commandment is revealed in beholding the promise that was from the beginning and was made immortal flesh in His Son Jesus Christ and being persuaded to believe on Him and His same life as your inheritance, so that you love one another, just as He gave commandment that you should partake of His life, standing before Him holy and without blame in love.

24 And he who allows himself to be served by Him with eternal life keeps His commandment and dwells in Him, and He in him. And this is how we know that His life abides in us, by His Spirit which He has given us.

Chapter 4

1 Beloved do not believe every teaching but test each doctrine whether it comes from the Spirit of God: for there are many false prophets in the world who claim to speak on behalf of God, speaking lies and deceiving many.

2 This is how you can know the Spirit of God: Every teaching that confesses that Jesus is the Christ; the Word of eternal life and has come out of the grave in immortal flesh is of God:

3 And every teaching that denies that Jesus Christ has come out of the grave in immortal flesh is not of God: this doctrine

stands completely opposed to the doctrine of Christ, which opposition, and deception you heard would come and even now is already in the world.

4 You are born of the Spirit of God, little children, and overcome the death and corruption in the world: because the Spirit of God that is in you is greater than the spirit in the world, having already made the same death and corruption in the world bow down in the body of Jesus Christ.

5 Those who are born from the wisdom in the world: will speak of all the corruptible things that are in the world through lust, and the world hears them.

6 We are born of God, born from above, and he who knows God, hears us; he who is not of God but of the world does not hear us. By this we know the Spirit of truth and the spirit in the world that is filled with lies and deceit departing from the Word that God has spoken in Christ and was made immortal flesh in the resurrection.

7 Beloved, let us abide in Him who is love so that we might love one another: for love abides with God and love is God and anyone who loves is born of God, and knows and is known by God.

8 He that does not love, does not abide in God, nor does he know God; for God is love.

9 This is how the love of God is revealed to us, in that God sent His Son, His only begotten Son, born of a woman, born of the Spirit, who laid down His life for us and has become the firstborn from the dead, immortal, so that in and through Him we might have that same incorruptible life.

10 Herein is love, not that you love God, but that God loves you. And because of His great love for you, desiring to be good to you for all the ages to come, He did not want you to perish in death but He has shown Himself favorable towards you in the Son, conquering the death that all your lifetime had you subject to fear and torment.

11 Beloved, if God who is the source of love has so loved us, serving us with who He is, abiding in His love allows us to love one another just as He has loved us.

12 No man has seen God at any time. When we love one another, we experience intimacy with the love of God that abides in us toward others, and His love is perfected in us to know and be known of Him.

13 This is how we know that we are in Him and He is in us because His Spirit lives in us testifying to us that we are the sons of God.

14 And we have seen with our own eyes and testify now to you that the Father sent the Son to be the Savior of the world and He has become the author of eternal salvation unto all them who believe.

15 Whosoever is persuaded and believes that Jesus is the Son of God, has not received this by flesh and blood but has been revealed this incorruptible word by The Spirit of God which dwells and remains in him, and he in God.

16 And in Him have we known and believed the love that God has towards us. For God is love, the very source of love, and he that abides in Him, abides in love, and God abides in him.

17 Herein is the love of God made perfect in our hearts, so that we will be able to stand in boldness before Him in the day of judgment; being persuaded that He could never be pleased that we were dead and perishing, but could only be satisfied in sharing His life with us, and being good to us forever, being confident that just as Jesus Christ is the Son of God clothed with glory and honor from the Father, so are you in this world.

18 There is no fear of death in the love of God that He has spoken to us in Christ, the Word of life that came out of the grave in immortal flesh, but abiding in His perfect love, casts out the source of all fear from our hearts: because the fear of death is the thing that has brought torment and kept us in bondage all our days, for he who fears is not abiding in the perfect love of God that has conquered his death.

19 We love Him because He first showed Himself loving toward us in Christ; the Word of eternal life, in conquering our death.

20 If a man says he loves God and hates his brother, he is not walking in the truth of the Word of eternal life but in the lie

that is born from death: for if he does not see how God has so loved both him and his brother in conquering their death in the body of Jesus Christ, Whom he can see, how can he say he loves God who's love can only be seen in Christ?

21 And this eternal life that we have been given and has been revealed in immortal flesh, is the only life where we love God and love our brother also.

Chapter 5

1 Whosoever believes that Jesus is the Christ; the Word of eternal life which has come from the heart of the Father and was made immortal flesh in the resurrection, is born of God and has loved God: and everyone that loves the Father who fathered the Son, also loves the Son who is fathered of Him; for just as they are One flesh, so may we also, be one with Him.

2 By this union do we know that we love the children of God, for when we love God, we keep His commandment and are kept by Him in His eternal life.

3 For in this is the love of God revealed; eternal life, so that we keep and are kept by abiding in His commandment: and His commandment is not grievous, because it is not a life that we need to bring forth in our own strength but the life wherein we allow Him to serve us with His life that is without end.

4 For whatsoever is born from the Word of eternal life that God has spoken in Christ, overcomes the death and corruption in the world: and this testimony, is the strength and the victory over the death in the world, the faith of the Son of God that is in our heart.

5 Who is the one that overcomes the death in the world, but the one who believes that Jesus is the Son of God?

6 This is He that came in the flesh, born of a virgin, born of the Spirit, the Lord from heaven, being baptized by water into our death and by the faith contained in the shedding of His blood, The Son of God, Jesus Christ; who has not just come by water but has thoroughly washed away our death in His

219

blood. And the Holy Spirit who descended upon Him when a voice came from heaven bearing witness saying, "You are My beloved Son in You I am well pleased"; whose testimony is true because the Spirit is the Spirit of truth.

7 For there are three that bear record in heaven that He is the Son of God, the Father, the Word of God, and the Holy Ghost: and their record is faithful and true and these three are one.

8 And there are three that bear witness to us in the earth, the Spirit, that we are also the sons of God, and the water, that we are buried in the baptism of His death and so shall we be raised up with Him, and the blood, that death has been conquered in His flesh: and these three agree in one.

9 If we receive testimony from men surely the testimony of God is greater: and the witness that God has testified about us is found in His Son.

10 He that believes on the Son of God has seen himself in the testimony that God gave in the Son. He that believes not in the testimony given in the Son has made God out to be a liar; because he has not believed the witness that God has sent to testify of him.

11 And this is the testimony that God has given about us in the Son, Eternal life, the same life He promised from the beginning and is in immortal flesh in the Son at His right hand.

12 He that has the testimony of the Son, has the Son and the same life that is in the Son, and he that does not receive that witness in himself has no life, for there is no other life.

13 These things I have written to you who believe on the name of the Son of God; in the life and inheritance that God has promised and given you in the Son so that you can be certain that you have eternal life, the same life in the Son, that you might know that you have been surnamed by God His son: believing in the name of the Son of God.

14 And as His sons, this is the confidence that we have in Him, that all He has in Himself is ours and so if we ask, He hears us:

15 And knowing that He hears us and has given us everything that our hearts have ever desired, we can be certain that whatever we ask we have received the thing that we truly desire of Him.

16 If a man sees any of his brothers overtaken in a fault which does not lead to them perishing in death, he can ask, and God will restore unto life them that are taken in a fault not unto death. There is a way in the heart of a man that denies and rejects God's life for his own way, that is the iniquity that perishes in death and I do not say that you can pray for it.

17 All the evil works that death has brought and stung the heart of man with, that would cause them to perish in their own destruction and iniquity are unjust. And there are works not of faith that do not perish in death.

18 We know that whoever is born from the Word of eternal life made immortal flesh, no longer labors to establish his own corruptible life but his flesh goes to rest in God's life and immortality, and the peace of God keeps him abiding in that word so that the corruption in the world touches him not.

19 And we know that we are the sons of God, fathered by Him and know that all that is in the entire world is that which serves men with the corruption and death brought by the wicked one.

20 And we know that the Son of God has come and given us all the treasures of wisdom and understanding to discern what is born from life and of death, so that we may know Him in truth, that we may abide in Him in the truth, even in His Son. This is the true God and eternal life so that we may have fellowship with the Father and His Son Jesus Christ.

21 Little children, keep yourself abiding in the love of God that is revealed in the Word of eternal life, where you find life and peace, no longer under the bondage of death and the fear of death and it will keep your heart from looking to that which the world can give you. Amen.

The Second Epistle of

JOHN

The Faith Translation

Chapter 1

1 John the elder to the elect lady and her children, who I love fellowshipping together with the Father and His Son Jesus Christ, abiding in eternal life, along with all that have known the truth,

2 Because of the truth of eternal life abiding in us and with us for all the ages to come.

3 And His grace which will be with us always, in all mercy and peace, from God the Father and from the Lord Jesus Christ, the Son of the Father who keeps us in truth and love.

4 I greatly rejoice that I have found your children abiding in the truth of eternal life, which is the decree and the testimony we have received in Christ from the Father.

5 And now I urge you also, lady, that you abide in the truth, not as if it is some new commandment to you, but rather the same commandment of eternal life that was from the beginning, so that we love one another in the truth.

6 And this is how His love is born in us that we have love one for another, through abiding in His life as He gave command. This eternal life is the only command which you have heard from the beginning, that you should abide therein.

7 For there are many deceivers in the world, who say that Jesus Christ did not come as a man, coming out of the grave in immortal flesh, who deny that He is the Word of eternal life to those in dying flesh. This is a deception and oppose to the doctrine of Christ.

8 Take heed of this message which stands oppose Christ and do not be lazy with the truth but diligent, so that our labor is not in vain but rather receive the message that has a full reward.

9 Whoever rejects Christ, denies the wisdom and the power of God that conquered death in human flesh, and transgresses the way unto life for all flesh and does not abide in the doctrine of Christ and has not God. He that abides in the doctrine of Christ, has both the Father and the Son abiding in him.

10 If anyone comes to your house teaching this doctrine that is oppose to Christ, do not allow it, neither rejoice with him or do anything that would be seen as an endorsement.

11 Because whoever allows this message and rejoices with him has been lazy with the truth and taken part in that which only brings corruption and pain to men's lives.

12 I have many things to write to you that I would not write with paper and ink: but I hope to come to you, that we may speak face to face, and that our joy may be full.

13 The children of your elect sister greet you. Amen.

The Third Epistle of

JOHN

The Faith Translation

Chapter 1

1 The elder John to the well-beloved Ga'ius, who I love (*and fellowship with*) in the truth.

2 Beloved, I pray (*that this letter finds*) you well, flourishing in every way in your life; both sound in mind and healthy in body, in the same way (*that I hear*) your soul is prospering (*with the fruit of eternal life*).

3 Because I rejoiced immensely upon hearing the brethren who came and testified (*to me*) of the truth that they see (*is alive*) in you, even (*as you just live your life*) you walk (*effortlessly*) in the truth (*of His life in you*).

4 I have no greater joy than to hear that my children (*who I have fathered in the word of eternal life*) walk in the truth.

5 Beloved, the work that you do in your ministry, wherein on every occasion you speak to impart the faith and the love of God to the brethren, you also do the same to strangers;

6 Who have borne witness regarding your love before the church (*at Ephesus*): to whom you have built up in the truth (*that they are as they ought to be, accepted and loved*) so that they might prosper in their journey; you have done a beautiful thing:

7 And because (*you have shown them the love and grace He has toward them*) they have gone forward (*depending*) on His name's sake alone, not having to take any (*support*) from the Gentiles.

8 We (*who have a desire in our hearts to see the truth of the gospel proclaimed*) should receive such men, so that we also might be fellow helpers (*like you*) in declaring the truth.

9 I wrote to the church myself: but Di-ot-re-phes, who aspires to have preeminence (*lording over*), and desiring the chief place of influence among those in the church, did not receive us.

10 Because of this, if I come, I will bring to your remembrance the thing that he has done, coming against us (*who receive such men with joy*) with his idle accusations and use of malicious words: and who not being satisfied (*and finding fault*) with these men, not only does he flat out forbid and not

receive the brethren and strangers from coming but he also (*seeks to use his influence to*) throw out those who do (*receive them*) from the church.

11 Beloved do not follow after (*by trying to imitate*) the way which poisons from within, which is evil but rather (*be persuaded by that which originates with God*) which is good. For he that (*is persuaded by God*) does good because he is born from the life of God: but he that (*labors to establish his own life and preeminence*) does evil and has not seen God (*neither is His word abiding in him*).

12 De-me-tri-us has a good report of all men (*who are to be received with gladness*), and (*whose testimony is born*) from the truth itself: yes, and we also bear record of the same; and you can be certain that our record is true (*because it is found in the record that God gave in His Son, Jesus Christ*).

13 I had many things to write, but I will not write them to you with ink and pen:

14 But I hope that I will see you shortly, and we will speak face to face (*and you can hear these words from my own mouth*). Peace be to you. All our friends here salute you. Greet all my friends there with you by name.

The General Epistle of

JUDE

The Faith Translation

Chapter 1

1 Jude, who willingly belongs to Jesus Christ, the brother of James, to those who have been set apart and loved by God the Father, kept perfectly in Jesus Christ, and surnamed His sons,

2 His tender compassion toward you, and peace and love be multiplied to you.

3 Beloved, when I was compelled to write to you concerning the salvation in which we share, it became absolutely necessary for me to write, and urge you that you should diligently contend for (*and declare*) the faith which was once and for all time delivered to the saints in Jesus Christ.

4 Because certain men have come in stealthily, who are walking in the way that God has judged from the beginning only brings corruption and death, ungodly men who exchange the judgment of God in Christ to give us blessing and life as a gift into an unbridled lust for life through the strength contained in their flesh and rejecting the life of the only Lord God and our Lord Jesus Christ.

5 I will remind you, though you once knew this, how the Lord, who saved His people out of the bondage of Egypt, by His strength alone, which people afterward forsook the judgment and promise of God for their own way, utterly perished in the wilderness in their unbelief in His promise to give them the land as a gift.

6 And the angels which kept not their original design but forsook their habitation for darkness are now bound in everlasting chains under the judgment of darkness of that great day.

7 Just as Sodom and Gomorrah also exchanged the life of their design and went a whoring after other gods, and were given over to their desire for vile sexual activity with different flesh, serve as an example to us, heaping unto themselves suffering, having gone out of the way that leads to life, but continued in the way God judged from the beginning could only bring them grief and sorrow, destruction, and death.

8 Likewise those who have crept in are beguiled in their imaginations of the life they can bring forth in their own strength, which way defiles their flesh; having rejected and set aside divine judgment, they are not afraid to speak against God or man.

9 Yet not even Michael the archangel when he disputed with the accuser, over whether the body of Moses belonged to the Lord, dared not bring an accusation of his own but simply said, the Lord's judgment is against you.

10 But these men speak their own private judgments (*and interpretations*) of those things which they have no intimate knowledge: but rather having become intimately acquainted with their own fleshly desires they have become like wild beasts, not human (*void of all rational thought and judgment*) who bring corruption upon themselves.

11 Woe to them! For they have gone the same way as Cain (*whose work to establish his own life by the fruit he could gather to himself, God judged as unjust and that which leads to backbiting, jealousy, and murder*), and like Balaam they have rushed unrestrained in their lust for life for the reward which they can serve themselves, and perish the same way as Korah, by standing opposed to the judgment of God unto life.

12 These are the ones who secretly sit with you in your feasts of love, and when you take the Lord's supper, but all the while they are feeding their bellies with their flesh, having no reverence to the way of the Lord unto life, not eating from the table prepared by the Lord. They are empty vessels, tossed around by the wind, trees whose fruit withers, and is scorched by the heat, bearing no fruit, and are twice dead, (*having been delivered from Adam's death, they are now dead in their own iniquity*), and plucked up by the roots;

13 Raging waves tossed by the sea that find no rest, but continually spue out their own shame; stars void of light that wander aimlessly, who heap to themselves despair and the certainty of the blackness of darkness forever.

14 And Enoch, the seventh from Adam, also prophesied of these, saying, Behold, when the Lord Jesus comes with tens of thousands of His saints,

15 To bring the justice (*of His life*) to all His beloved, and (*the brightness of His countenance*) lays bare the secrets in the heart of those who have given no reverence to the way that (*God has judged*) leads to life that stand among them, it will reveal that it is their own works they have worked that bring shame and condemnation to their hearts (*not God who condemns them*), and proving that their hard words (*have only brought labors and annoyances*) which words they have spoken contrary to Him who gives His blessing and life as a gift.

16 These are grumblers (*and complainers*) who blame others for their discontentment, and live by their unquenchable appetite (*to do, to get and to have*) life through the strength contained in their flesh (*never finding satisfaction*); and their mouth speaks greatly exaggerated and flattering words that advance their own agenda with rich and educated men who they hold in high regard in order to gain money, influence and power.

17 But I call to your remembrance beloved, the words which were spoken before by the apostles (*Paul and Peter*) of our Lord Jesus Christ;

18 How that they told you there would be false teachers in the last days (*of death in the earth*) who will depart from the faith of our Lord Jesus Christ, and (*instead*) will walk after their own lust (*to do, to get and to have life*) by the strength contained in their flesh.

19 These are those who cause division, who teach and are mindful of the principles contained in the world (*of touch not, taste not, handle not and the practice of will worship*), having not the Spirit of God.

20 But you who have the Spirit (*who is always pointing to the faith contained in Jesus Christ*) are built up in the inner man, being persuaded (*that being dead to death you are alive to God*) that you are set apart unto His same life, always speaking in

and listening to the Holy Ghost (*as He comforts you of the certainty of that life*),

21 Whereby (*He keeps you*) abiding in the love of God, and (*there is no occasion of stumbling*) where you continually (*fellowship with Him*) looking for the comfort only He can bring (*from the corruption in the world*) through the mercy and loving kindness of our Lord Jesus Christ unto eternal life (*and bodily immortality*).

22 And some will teach the loving compassion of our Lord Jesus, (*by declaring the faith of Him*) making a difference (*to others*):

23 Who will be snatched (*like a brand plucked*) from the fire; and hating (*the perishable life in the world*), and the spotted garment of their body of death (*will He clothe upon them with His incorruptible life*).

24 Now to Him who is able to keep you from falling (*so that you will not cower away in fear*), but present you faultless (*undefiled and without blame, in His life and immortality*) before the presence of His glory with exceeding joy,

25 To the God of all wisdom our Savior, be glory and majesty, dominion, and power, both right now and forever. Amen.

Made in the USA
Middletown, DE
15 September 2023

38519289R00130